SLOW COOK

Contents

Welcome!

Not only am I a dedicated and enthusiastic cook, but I love nothing more than encouraging those who think they are domestically challenged to pick up a pan and a spoon and get stirring. It doesn't take much to grasp the basics and from there, anything is possible. Hiding behind the mantra 'I can't cook' only brings fear into the kitchen, but it is these mistakes that will ultimately make you a better, more confident and knowledgeable cook. All it takes is some good recipes and plenty of enthusiasm and kitchen domination will surely follow. Luckily, all Good Housekeeping cookery books are filled with tempting recipes with clear methods and realistic photography – we are taking the chance out of cooking as our recipes are guaranteed to work.

If you have ever tried turning the page of a cookery book with dirty hands, while also balancing a steaming pan and a sticky spoon, then you will love the flip-chart design of this book. The simple fact that the recipes stand upright makes for an easier cooking experience – say goodbye to hovering over recipes while trying to stop the spoon dripping on to the pages.

This Good Housekeeping Flip It! book collection is filled with meticulously triple-tested recipes that have been developed and put through their paces in our dedicated test kitchens. We hope you enjoy the recipes and that they inspire you to give them a try – you know that they'll work after all!

Meike.

Cookery Editor
Good Housekeeping

Spiced Bean & Vegetable Stew

Serves 6
Preparation Time
15 minutes
Cooking Time
10 minutes in pan
then 2–3 hours
on Low

Per Serving
262 calories
7g fat
(of which 1g saturates)
44g carbohydrate
1.3g salt

Vegetarian
Gluten Free Dairy Free

3 tbsp olive oil
2 small onions, sliced
2 garlic cloves, crushed
1 tbsp sweet paprika
1 small dried red chilli, seeded and finely chopped
(see Cook's Tip, page 37)
700g (1½lb) sweet potatoes, cubed
700g (1½lb) pumpkin, cut into chunks
125g (4oz) okra, trimmed
500g passata
400g can haricot or cannellini beans,
drained and rinsed
450ml (¾ pint) hot vegetable stock
(see Cook's Tip, page 69)
salt and ground black pepper

1 Heat the oil in a large pan over a very gentle heat. Add the onions and garlic and cook for 5 minutes.

2 Stir in the paprika and chilli and cook for 2 minutes, then add the sweet potatoes, pumpkin, okra, passata, beans and hot stock. Season generously with salt and pepper and bring to the boil.

3 Transfer to the slow cooker, cover and cook on Low for 2–3 hours until the vegetables are tender.

Without a Slow Cooker
Complete the recipe to the end of step 2, but leaving out the beans. Cover the pan and simmer for 20 minutes or until the vegetables are tender. Add the beans and cook for 3 minutes to warm through. Serve immediately.

Try Something Different
Instead of paprika, use 1 tsp each ground cumin and ground coriander. Garnish with freshly chopped coriander and serve.

Mushroom & Bean Hotpot

Serves 6
Preparation Time
15 minutes
Cooking Time
15 minutes in pan
then 2–3 hours
on Low

Per Serving
280 calories
10g fat
(of which 1g saturates)
34g carbohydrate
1.3g salt

Vegetarian
Gluten Free

3 tbsp olive oil
700g (1½lb) chestnut mushrooms, roughly chopped
1 large onion, finely chopped
2 tbsp plain flour
2 tbsp mild curry paste
150ml (¼ pint) dry white wine
1 × 400g can chopped tomatoes
2 tbsp sun-dried tomato paste
2 × 400g cans mixed beans, drained and rinsed
3 tbsp mango chutney
3 tbsp freshly chopped coriander and mint

1 Heat the oil in a large pan over a low heat. Add the mushrooms and onion and fry until the onion is soft and dark golden. Stir in the flour and curry paste and cook for 1–2 minutes, then add the wine, tomatoes, sun-dried tomato paste and beans.

2 Bring to the boil, then transfer to the slow cooker. Cover and cook on Low for 2–3 hours.

3 Stir in the chutney and herbs and serve.

Without a Slow Cooker
At the start of step 2, leave the mixture in the pan, bring to the boil, then reduce the heat and simmer for 30 minutes or until most of the liquid has reduced. Complete step 3 to finish the recipe.

Ratatouille

Serves 6	4 tbsp olive oil
Preparation Time	2 onions, thinly sliced
20 minutes	1 large garlic clove, crushed
Cooking Time	350g (12oz) small aubergines, thinly sliced
15 minutes in pan	450g (1lb) small courgettes, thinly sliced
then 3–4 hours	450g (1lb) tomatoes, skinned, seeded and
on High	roughly chopped
	1 green and 1 red pepper, each cored, seeded
Per Serving	and sliced
150 calories	1 tbsp freshly chopped basil
9g fat	2 tsp freshly chopped thyme
(of which 1g saturates)	2 tbsp freshly chopped flat-leafed parsley
15g carbohydrate	2 tbsp sun-dried tomato paste
0.1g salt	salt and ground black pepper
Vegetarian	
Gluten Free Dairy Free	

1 Heat the oil in a large pan. Add the onions and garlic and fry gently for 10 minutes or until softened and golden.

2 Add the aubergines, courgettes, tomatoes, sliced peppers, herbs, tomato paste and seasoning. Fry, stirring, for 2–3 minutes.

3 Transfer to the slow cooker and cover. Cook on High for 3–4 hours until all the vegetables are tender. Taste and adjust the seasoning. Serve the ratatouille hot or at room temperature

Without a Slow Cooker
At the start of step 3, leave the mixture in the pan, cover tightly and simmer for 30 minutes or until all the vegetables are tender. Uncover towards the end if there is too much liquid. Season and serve as described in step 3.

Braised Chicory in White Wine

Serves 4
Preparation Time
5 minutes
Cooking Time
2–3 hours on Low

Per Serving
80 calories
7g fat
(of which 5g saturates)
3g carbohydrate
0.1g salt

Vegetarian
Gluten Free

50g (2oz) butter, softened
6 heads of chicory, trimmed
juice of ½ lemon
salt and ground black pepper
100ml (3½fl oz) white wine
snipped fresh chives to serve

1 Grease the slow cooker dish with 15g (½oz) butter. Toss the chicory in the lemon juice and lay in the base of the dish.

2 Season to taste, add the wine and dot the remaining butter over the top. Cover and cook on Low for 2–3 hours until soft. Scatter with chives to serve.

Without a Slow Cooker
Grease a 1.7 litre (3 pint) ovenproof dish instead of the slow cooker. Cover with foil and cook in the oven for 1 hour until soft.

Braised Red Cabbage

Serves 8
Preparation Time
10 minutes
Cooking Time
2-3 hours on Low

Per Serving
50 calories
trace fat
11g carbohydrate
0g salt

Vegetarian
Gluten Free Dairy Free

½ medium red cabbage, about 500g (1lb 2oz),
shredded
1 red onion, finely chopped
1 Bramley apple, peeled, cored and chopped
25g (1oz) light muscovado sugar
1 cinnamon stick
pinch of ground cloves
¼ tsp freshly grated nutmeg
2 tbsp each red wine vinegar and red wine
juice of 1 orange
salt and ground black pepper

1 Put all the ingredients into the slow cooker and stir to mix well. Cover and cook on Low for 2-3 hours.

2 When the cabbage is tender, remove the pan from the heat and discard the cinnamon stick. Serve at once, or leave to cool, then put into a bowl, cover and chill the cabbage overnight.

3 To reheat, put the cabbage into a pan, add 2 tbsp cold water and cover with a tight-fitting lid. Bring to the boil, then reduce the heat and simmer for 25 minutes.

Without a Slow Cooker
Heat 2 tbsp olive oil in a large heavy-based pan. Add the onion and cook gently for 3-4 minutes to soften. Add the cabbage, sugar, spices, vinegars and orange juice, and season well. Bring to the boil, reduce the heat, then cover the pan and simmer for 30 minutes. Add the apples and stir through. Cook for a further 15 minutes or until the cabbage is tender and nearly all the liquid has evaporated. Discard the cinnamon stick before serving.

Lentils with Red Pepper

Serves 4
Preparation Time
10 minutes
Cooking Time
20 minutes in pan
then 3–4 hours
on High

Per Serving
296 calories
5g fat
(of which 1g saturates)
47g carbohydrate
0.1g salt

Vegetarian
Gluten Free Dairy Free

1 tbsp olive oil
1 large onion, finely chopped
2 celery sticks, trimmed and diced
2 carrots, diced
2 bay leaves, torn
300g (11oz) Puy lentils
600ml (1 pint) hot vegetable stock
(see Cook's Tip, page 69)
1 marinated red pepper, drained
and chopped
2 tbsp freshly chopped flat-leafed parsley,
plus extra to garnish
ground black pepper

1 Heat the oil in a pan. Add the onion and cook over a low heat for 15 minutes or until soft. Add the celery, carrots and bay leaves and cook for 2 minutes.

2 Add the lentils with the hot stock and stir everything together. Transfer to the slow cooker, cover and cook on High for 3–4 hours.

3 Stir in the red pepper and parsley and season with pepper. Leave to stand for 10 minutes, then garnish with extra parsley and serve as an accompaniment.

Without a Slow Cooker
At the end of step 2, leave the mixture in the pan, half cover with a lid, and simmer over a low heat for 25–30 minutes. Complete the recipe from step 3.

Spiced Roast Turkey

Serves 8
Preparation Time
30 minutes
Cooking Time
3 hours,
plus resting

Per Serving
611 calories
40g fat
(of which 16g saturates)
12g carbohydrate
2.0g salt

4.5kg (10lb) oven-ready turkey
Pork, Spinach and Apple Stuffing, thawed if frozen
(see Cook's Tip)
2 tsp Cajun spice seasoning
150g (5oz) butter, softened
salt and ground black pepper
fresh herbs to garnish

For the sausages
8 sausages
16 thin streaky bacon rashers

1 Preheat the oven 190°C (170°C fan oven) mark 5. Loosen the skin at the neck end of the turkey, ease your fingers up between the skin and the breast and, using a small, sharp knife, remove the wishbone.

2 Season the inside of the turkey, then spoon the cold stuffing into the neck end only. Neaten the shape, turn the bird over and secure the neck skin with skewers or cocktail sticks.

3 Put the turkey into a roasting tin, mix the spice with the butter, smear it over the turkey and season. Cover with a tent of foil. Roast in the oven for about 3 hours, basting occasionally. If the legs were tied together, loosen after the first hour so that they cook more evenly.

4 Meanwhile, twist each sausage in half and cut to make two mini sausages. Stretch the bacon rashers by running the blunt side of a kitchen knife along each rasher (this stops them shrinking too much when they're cooked). Roll a rasher around each mini sausage. Put into a small roasting tin or around the turkey and cook for about 1 hour. Remove the foil from the turkey 45 minutes before the end of the cooking time.

5 To check whether the turkey is cooked, pierce the thickest part of the flesh with a skewer; the juices should run clear. If there is any sign of blood, cook for 10 minutes, then check again in the same way.

6 When the turkey is cooked, tip the bird so the juices run into the tin, then put it on a warmed serving plate with the sausages. Cover loosely with foil and leave to rest for 20–30 minutes before carving. Garnish with herbs.

Cook's Tip
Pork, Spinach and Apple Stuffing Heat 2 tbsp olive oil in a frying pan. Add 150g (5oz) finely chopped onion and cook for 10 minutes or until soft. Increase the heat, add 225g (8oz) fresh spinach (torn into pieces if the leaves are large) and cook until wilted. Add 2 sharp apples (such as Granny Smith), peeled, cored and cut into chunks, and cook, stirring, for 2–3 minutes, then leave to cool. When the mixture is cold, add 400g (14oz) pork sausagemeat, the coarsely grated zest of 1 lemon, 1 tbsp freshly chopped thyme, 100g (3½oz) fresh white breadcrumbs and 2 large eggs, beaten. Season with salt and ground black pepper and stir until evenly mixed. Serves 8.

Turkey Crown with Orange

Serves 8
Preparation Time
20 minutes
Cooking Time
2½ hours,
plus resting

Per Serving
181 calories
6g fat
(of which 3g saturates)
3g carbohydrate
0.2g salt

Gluten Free

2 onions, sliced
2 bay leaves
2.7kg (6lb) oven-ready turkey crown
40g (1½oz) butter, softened
1 lemon, halved
2 tbsp chicken seasoning
2 oranges, halved
150ml (¼ pint) dry white wine or chicken stock
(see Cook's Tip)

1 Preheat the oven to 190°C (170°C fan oven) mark 5. Spread the onions in a large roasting tin, add the bay leaves and sit the turkey on top. Spread the butter over the turkey breast, then squeeze the lemon over it. Put the lemon halves in the tin. Sprinkle the chicken seasoning over the turkey and then put the orange halves in the tin, around the turkey.

2 Pour the wine or stock into the roasting tin, with 250ml (9fl oz) hot water. Cover the turkey loosely with a large sheet of foil. Make sure it's completely covered, but with enough space between the foil and the turkey for air to circulate.

3 Roast in the oven for 2 hours or until the turkey is cooked through and the juices run clear when the thickest part of the thigh is pierced with a skewer. Remove the foil and put back in the oven for 30 minutes or until golden.

4 Lift the turkey on to a warmed carving dish, cover loosely with foil and leave to rest for 15 minutes before carving.

Cook's Tip
Chicken Stock To make chicken stock put 225g (8oz) roughly chopped onions, 150g (5oz) trimmed and roughly chopped leeks, 225g (8oz) roughly chopped celery sticks and 1.6kg (3½lb) raw chicken bones into a large pan with 3 litres (5¼ pints) cold water, 1 bouquet garni (2 bay leaves, a few fresh parsley and thyme sprigs) 1 tsp black peppercorns and ½ tsp sea salt. Bring slowly to the boil and skim the surface. Partially cover the pan, reduce the heat and simmer gently for 2 hours; check the seasoning. Strain the stock through a fine sieve into a bowl and cool quickly. Cover and keep in the fridge for up to three days. Remove the fat from the surface and use the stock as required. Makes 1.1 litres (2 pints).

Chicken with Chorizo & Beans

Serves 6

Preparation Time
10 minutes

Cooking Time
30 minutes in pan then
4–5 hours on Low

Per Serving
690 calories
41g fat
(of which 12g saturates)
33g carbohydrate
2.6g salt

Gluten Free Dairy Free

1 tbsp olive oil
12 chicken pieces (6 drumsticks and 6 thighs)
175g (6oz) chorizo sausage, cubed
1 onion, finely chopped
2 large garlic cloves, crushed
1 tsp mild chilli powder
3 red peppers, seeded and roughly chopped
400g (14oz) passata
2 tbsp tomato purée
150ml (¼ pint) hot chicken stock (see Cook's Tip, page 17)
2 × 400g cans butter beans, drained and rinsed
200g (7oz) new potatoes, quartered
small bunch of thyme
1 bay leaf
200g (7oz) baby leaf spinach

1 Heat the oil in a large pan over a medium heat. Add the chicken and fry until browned all over, then transfer to the slow cooker.

2 Add the chorizo to the pan and fry for 2–3 minutes until its oil starts to run. Add the onion, garlic and chilli powder and fry over a low heat for 5 minutes or until the onion is soft.

3 Add the red peppers and cook for 2–3 minutes until soft. Stir in the passata, tomato purée, hot stock, butter beans, potatoes, thyme sprigs and bay leaf. Bring to the boil, then add to the chicken. Cover and cook on Low for 4–5 hours until the chicken is cooked through.

4 Remove the thyme and bay leaf, then stir in the spinach until it wilts. Serve immediately.

Without a Slow Cooker
Preheat the oven to 190°C (170°C fan oven) mark 5. At the end of step 1, transfer the chicken to a plate, then complete step 2. Add all the ingredients as described in step 3, cover and simmer for 10 minutes. Return the chicken to the pan, bring to a simmer, then pour everything into an ovenproof casserole with a lid and cook for 30–35 minutes in the oven. Complete step 4 to finish the recipe.

Slow-braised Garlic Chicken

Serves 6

Preparation Time
30 minutes

Cooking Time
about 2 hours

Per Serving
506 calories
28g fat
(of which 9g saturates)
10g carbohydrate
1g salt

2 tbsp olive oil
1 tbsp freshly chopped thyme
125g (4oz) chestnut mushrooms,
finely chopped
6 whole chicken legs (drumsticks and thighs)
18 thin slices pancetta
2 tbsp plain flour
25g (1oz) butter
18 small shallots
12 garlic cloves, unpeeled but split
1 × 750ml bottle full-bodied white wine,
such as Chardonnay
2 bay leaves
salt and ground black pepper

1 Preheat the oven to 180°C (160°C fan oven) mark 4. Heat 1 tbsp oil in a frying pan. Add the thyme and mushrooms and fry until the moisture has evaporated. Season with salt and pepper and cool.

2 Loosen the skin away from one chicken leg and spoon a little of the mushroom paste underneath. Season the leg all over with salt and pepper, then wrap three pancetta slices around the thigh end. Repeat with the remaining chicken legs, then dust using 1 tbsp flour.

3 Melt the butter in a frying pan with the remaining oil over a high heat. Fry the chicken legs, in batches, seam side down, until golden. Turn the legs, brown the other side, then transfer to a casserole. The browning should take 8–10 minutes per batch.

4 Put the shallots and garlic into the frying pan and cook for 10 minutes or until browned. Sprinkle over the remaining flour and cook for 1 minute. Pour in the wine and bring to the boil, stirring. Pour into the casserole with the chicken and add the bay leaves. Cover and cook in the oven for 1½ hours. Serve hot.

Freezing Tip
To freeze Complete the recipe. Cool quickly, then freeze in an airtight container for up to one month.
To use Thaw overnight at cool room temperature. Preheat the oven to 220°C (200°C fan oven) mark 7. Put the chicken back into the casserole and reheat in the oven for 15 minutes. Reduce the oven temperature to 180°C (160°C fan oven) mark 4 and cook for a further 25 minutes.

Spanish Chicken

Serves 4	1 tsp ground turmeric
Preparation Time	1.1 litres (2 pints) hot chicken stock (see Cook's
25 minutes, plus	Tip, page 17)
infusing	2 tbsp vegetable oil
Cooking Time	4 boneless, skinless chicken thighs, roughly diced
20 minutes in pan	1 onion, chopped
then 1–2 hours	1 red pepper, seeded and sliced
on Low	50g (2oz) chorizo sausage, diced
	2 garlic cloves, crushed
Per Serving	300g (11oz) long-grain rice
671 calories	125g (4oz) frozen peas
28g fat	salt and ground black pepper
(of which 5g saturates)	3 tbsp freshly chopped flat-leafed parsley
70g carbohydrate	to garnish
0.8g salt	crusty bread to serve

Gluten Free Dairy Free

1 Add the turmeric to the hot stock and leave to infuse for at least 5 minutes. Meanwhile, heat the oil in a large frying pan over a medium heat. Add the chicken and fry for 10 minutes or until golden, then transfer to the slow cooker.

2 Add the onion to the pan and cook over a medium heat for 5 minutes or until soft. Add the red pepper and chorizo and cook for a further 5 minutes, then add the garlic and cook for 1 minute.

3 Add the rice and mix well. Pour in the stock and peas and season, then transfer to the slow cooker and stir together. Cover and cook on Low for 1–2 hours until the rice is tender and the chicken is cooked through.

4 Check the seasoning and garnish with the parsley. Serve with crusty bread.

Without a Slow Cooker

Complete step 1, setting the chicken aside on a plate. At the end of step 2, return the chicken to the pan, add the rice and one-third of the stock, then mix well and simmer until the liquid has been absorbed. Add the rest of the stock, along with the peas, bring to the boil, then reduce the heat to low and cook for 15–20 minutes until no liquid remains. Complete step 4 to finish the recipe.

Classic Coq au Vin

Serves 6	
Preparation Time	
15 minutes	
Cooking Time	
2 hours 10 minutes	
Per Serving	
740 calories	
44g fat	
(of which 17g saturates)	
26g carbohydrate	
1.8g salt	

1 large chicken, jointed, (see Cook's Tip)
or 6–8 chicken joints
2 tbsp well-seasoned flour
100g (3½oz) butter
125g (4oz) lean bacon, diced
1 medium onion, quartered
1 medium carrot, quartered
4 tbsp brandy
600ml (1 pint) red wine
1 garlic clove, crushed
1 bouquet garni (see Cook's Tip, page 73)
1 sugar cube
2 tbsp vegetable oil
450g (1lb) button onions
pinch of sugar
1 tsp wine vinegar
225g (8oz) button mushrooms
6 slices white bread, crusts removed
salt and ground black pepper

1 Coat the chicken pieces with 1 tbsp seasoned flour. Melt 25g (1oz) butter in a flameproof casserole. Add the chicken and fry until golden brown on all sides. Add the bacon, onion and carrot and fry until softened.

2 Heat the brandy in a small pan, pour over the chicken and ignite, shaking the pan. Pour in the wine and stir to dislodge any sediment from the base of the casserole. Add the garlic, bouquet garni and sugar cube and bring to the boil. Reduce the heat, cover and simmer for 1–1½ hours or until the chicken is cooked through.

3 Meanwhile, melt 25g (1oz) butter with 1 tsp oil in a frying pan. Add the button onions and fry until they begin to brown. Add the pinch of sugar and vinegar together with 1 tbsp water. Cover and simmer for 10–15 minutes until just tender. Keep warm.

4 Melt 25g (1oz) butter with 2 tsp oil in a pan. Add the mushrooms and cook for a few minutes, then turn off the heat and keep warm. Remove the chicken from the casserole and place in a dish. Surround with the onions and mushrooms and keep hot.

5 Discard the bouquet garni. Skim the excess fat from the cooking liquid, then boil for 3–5 minutes until reduced. Add the remaining oil to the fat in the frying pan and fry the bread until golden brown on both sides. Cut each slice into triangles.

6 Work the remaining butter and flour to make a beurre manié. Remove the casserole from the heat and add small pieces of the beurre manié to the liquid. Stir until smooth, then bring just to the boil. The sauce should be thick and shiny. Take off the heat and season. Return the chicken, onions and mushrooms to the casserole and stir. Serve with fried bread.

Cook's Tip
To joint a chicken, cut out the wishbone and remove wings. Remove wing tips. With the tail pointing towards you and breast side up, pull one leg away and cut through skin between leg and breast. Pull leg down until you crack joint between thigh bone and ribcage. Cut through then cut through remaining leg meat. Repeat on other side. To remove the breast with bone in, make a cut along the full length of breastbone. Cut through breastbone, then cut through ribcage following outline of breast meat. Repeat on other side. Trim off any flaps of skin or fat.

Chicken Tagine

Serves 4
Preparation Time
10 minutes
Cooking Time
20 minutes in the
pan then 4–5 hours
on Low

Per Serving
376 calories
22g fat
(of which 4g saturates)
19g carbohydrate
0.5g salt

Gluten Free Dairy Free

2 tbsp olive oil
4 chicken thighs
1 onion, chopped
2 tsp ground cinnamon
2 tbsp runny honey
150g (5oz) dried apricots
75g (3oz) blanched almonds
125ml (4fl oz) hot chicken stock
(see Cook's Tip, page 17)
salt and ground black pepper
flaked almonds to garnish
couscous to serve

1 Heat 1 tbsp oil in a large pan over a medium heat. Add the chicken and fry for 5 minutes or until brown, then transfer to the slow cooker.

2 Add the onion to the pan with the remaining oil and fry for 10 minutes or until softened.

3 Add the cinnamon, honey, apricots, almonds and hot stock to the onion and season well. Bring to the boil, then transfer to the slow cooker, cover and cook on Low for 4–5 hours until the chicken is tender and cooked through. Garnish with the flaked almonds and serve hot with couscous.

Without a Slow Cooker
Cook the tagine in a large, flameproof casserole. After step 1, transfer the chicken to a plate, complete step 2, then return the chicken to the casserole and add the ingredients as described at the start of step 3. Cover and bring to the boil, then reduce the heat and simmer for 45 minutes until the chicken is falling off the bone. Garnish and serve as described.

Stoved Chicken

Serves 4
Preparation Time
15 minutes
Cooking Time
about 2½ hours

Per serving
854 calories
45g fat
(of which 14g saturates)
55g carbohydrates
3g salt

25g (1oz) butter, plus a little extra
1 tbsp vegetable oil
4 chicken quarters, halved
125g (4oz) lean back bacon,
rind removed and chopped
1.1kg (2½lb) floury potatoes,
such as King Edward, peeled
and cut into 5mm (¼in) slices
2 large onions, sliced
2 tsp freshly chopped thyme
or ½ tsp dried thyme
600ml (1 pint) hot chicken stock
(see Cook's Tip, page 17)
salt and ground black pepper
snipped fresh chives to garnish

1 Preheat the oven to 150°C (130°C fan oven) mark 2. Heat half the butter and the oil in a large frying pan and fry the chicken and bacon for 5 minutes or until lightly browned.

2 Layer half the potato slices, then half the onion slices in the base of a large casserole. Season well, add the thyme and dot with half the remaining butter.

3 Add the chicken and bacon, season to taste and dot with the remaining butter. Cover with the remaining onions and finally a layer of potatoes. Season and dot with a little more butter. Pour the hot stock over.

4 Cover and cook in the oven for about 2½ hours or until the chicken is tender and the potatoes are cooked, adding a little more hot stock if necessary.

5 Just before serving sprinkle with snipped chives.

Goose with Roasted Apples

Serves 8
Preparation Time
30 minutes
Cooking Time
3 hours,
plus resting

Per Serving
646 calories
41g fat
(of which 12g saturates)
11g carbohydrate
1g salt

Dairy Free

6 small red onions, halved
7 small red eating apples, unpeeled, halved
5kg (11lb) oven-ready goose, washed, dried
and seasoned inside and out
small bunch of sage
small bunch of rosemary
1 bay leaf
salt and ground black pepper

For the gravy
1 tbsp plain flour
300ml (½ pint) red wine
200ml (7fl oz) giblet stock

1 Preheat the oven to 230°C (210°C fan oven) mark 8. Put half an onion and half an apple inside the goose with half the sage and rosemary and the bay leaf. Tie the legs together with string. Push a long skewer through the wings to tuck them in. Put the goose, breast side up, on a rack in a roasting tin. Prick the breast all over and season with salt and pepper. Put the remaining onions around the bird, then cover with foil.

2 Roast in the oven for 30 minutes, then remove the tin from the oven and baste the goose with the fat that has run off. Remove and set aside any excess fat. Reduce the oven temperature to 190°C (170°C fan oven) mark 5 and roast for a further 1½ hours, removing any excess fat every 20–30 minutes.

3 Remove the foil from the goose. Remove excess fat, then add the remaining apples. Sprinkle the goose with the remaining herbs and roast for a further 1 hour or until cooked. Test by piercing the thigh with a skewer – the juices should run clear. Remove the goose from the oven and put it on a warmed serving plate. Cover with foil and leave to rest for 30 minutes. Remove the apples and onions and keep warm.

4 To make the gravy, pour out all but 1 tbsp of the fat from the tin, stir in the flour, then add the wine and stock. Bring to the boil and cook, stirring, for 5 minutes. Carve the goose, cut the roast apples into wedges and serve with the goose, onions and gravy.

Duck Terrine with Apple, Apricot & Brandy

Serves 15
Preparation Time
1½ hours, plus
marinating
Cooking Time
2¼–2½ hours,
plus chilling

Per slice
189 calories
9g fat
(of which 3g saturates)
6g carbohydrates
0.3g salt

50g (2oz) stoned prunes, roughly chopped
(see Cook's Tips)
50g (2oz) ready-to-eat dried apricots,
roughly chopped (see Cook's Tips)
6 tbsp brandy
350g (12oz) turkey breast fillet, cut into 2.5cm
(1in) cubes
800g (1lb 12oz) duck breasts, skinned –
there should be 500g (1lb 2oz) meat
a few fresh thyme sprigs
50g (2oz) butter
225g (8oz) shallots or onions, roughly chopped
350g (12oz) eating apples, peeled, cored and chopped
225g (8oz) minced pork
2 tbsp freshly chopped thyme
1 medium egg, beaten
50g (2oz) shelled pistachio nuts
salt and ground black pepper
red onion chutney and bread to serve

1 The day before, put the prunes and apricots into a bowl with 4 tbsp of the brandy, cover and leave to soak overnight. Put the turkey and duck in a roasting tin at separate ends, sprinkle with the thyme sprigs and the remaining brandy, then cover and leave to marinate in the fridge overnight.

2 Heat the butter in a pan. Add the shallots and cook for 10 minutes or until soft. Stir in the apples, then cover and cook for 5–10 minutes until soft. Put to one side to cool.

3 Preheat the oven to 180°C (160°C fan oven) mark 4. Remove the turkey from the marinade and put into a food processor with the apple mixture and the minced pork. Whiz to a rough purée, then combine with the chopped thyme, egg, marinated fruits and the pistachio nuts. Season well with ½ tsp salt and a good grinding of pepper.

4 Remove the duck from the marinade and put between sheets of greaseproof paper. Flatten gently with a rolling pin until 1cm (½in) thick.

5 Base-line a 1.1 litre (2 pint) terrine or loaf tin with greaseproof paper or foil. Put a duck breast in the base of the terrine to cover it evenly with no gaps. Spread half the stuffing over it, then repeat the process, finishing with a layer of duck.

6 Cover with foil and put into a roasting tin. Add enough hot water to come three-quarters of the way up the sides of the terrine and cook in the oven for 2–2¼ hours until the juices run clear when tested with a skewer. Transfer to a wire rack, cover with a weighted board and, when cool, leave to chill for 6 hours or overnight.

7 Run a knife around the terrine and turn out on to a board. Remove the greaseproof paper and carve into thin slices. Serve with a red onion chutney and bread.

Cook's Tips
Try this with other dried fruit, such as dried cherries. You'll need 125g (4oz) in place of the prunes and apricots. Slicing this terrine, and any other terrine, is always easiest using a serrated knife.

Fruity Guinea Fowl

Serves 6	225g (8oz) onion, roughly chopped
Preparation Time	125g (4oz) each carrot and celery, chopped
40 minutes,	6–8 guinea fowl joints, 2kg (4½lb) total weight
plus marinating	750ml (1¼ pints) red wine
Cooking Time	1 tsp black peppercorns, crushed
4-6 hours on Low	1 tbsp freshly chopped thyme
	2 bay leaves
Per Serving	175g (6oz) ready-to-eat dried prunes
811 calories	3 tbsp vegetable oil
49g fat	225g (8oz) streaky bacon, cut into strips
(of which 14g saturates)	3 garlic cloves, crushed
24g carbohydrate	1 tsp harissa paste
1.7g salt	1 tbsp tomato purée
	2 tbsp plain flour
Dairy Free	300ml (½ pint) chicken stock
	(see Cook's Tip, page 17)
	2 apples, cored and sliced
	salt and ground black pepper
	mashed potatoes (see Cook's Tip, page 63) to serve

1 Put the onion, carrot, celery, guinea fowl, 600ml (1 pint) wine, the peppercorns, thyme and bay leaves into a large bowl. Cover, chill and leave to marinate for at least 3-4 hours. Soak the prunes in the remaining wine for 3-4 hours.

2 Preheat the oven to 170°C (150°C fan oven) mark 3. Drain and dry the joints (put the vegetables and wine to one side). Heat 2 tbsp oil in a large pan. Brown the joints in batches, over a medium heat, then transfer to the slow cooker.

3 Add the marinated vegetables and bacon to the pan (keep the marinade to one side) and stir-fry for 5 minutes. Add the garlic, harissa and tomato purée, and cook for 1 minute. Mix in the flour and cook for 1 minute. Pour in the reserved marinade and stock. Bring to the boil, stirring, then pour into the slow cooker. Season well. Cover and cook on Low for 4-6 hours until the guinea fowl is cooked through.

4 Heat the remaining oil in a pan. Cook the apples for 2-3 minutes on each side until golden. Put to one side. Remove the joints. Strain the sauce and return to the slow cooker with the joints. Add the prunes and any juices, and the apple. Leave to stand for 10 minutes. Serve with mashed potatoes.

Without a Slow Cooker
In step 2 set the joints to one side after browning, then continue with step 3 until you pour in the reserved marinade and stock. Bring to the boil, season well, cover and cook in the oven for 40 minutes. Complete the recipe from step 4, returning the sauces to the casserole instead of the slow cooker. Heat through in the oven for 10 minutes before serving.

Braised Guinea Fowl & Red Cabbage

Serves 8

Preparation Time
30 minutes

Cooking Time
2 hours 20 minutes

Per Serving
373 calories
17g fat
(of which 6g saturates)
12g carbohydrate
0.9g salt

Dairy Free

2 tbsp rapeseed oil
2 oven-ready guinea fowl
150g (5oz) smoked bacon lardons
400g (14oz) whole shallots, peeled
1 small red cabbage, cored and finely sliced
12 juniper berries, crushed
2 tsp dark brown sugar
1 tbsp red wine vinegar
2 fresh thyme sprigs
150ml (¼ pint) hot chicken stock
(see Cook's Tip, page 17)
salt and ground black pepper

1 Preheat the oven to 180°C (160°C fan oven) mark 4. Heat 1 tbsp oil in a flameproof casserole large enough for both birds and brown the guinea fowl over a medium to high heat. Remove from the casserole and put to one side.

2 Add the remaining oil to the casserole with the lardons. Fry gently to release the fat, then add the shallots and cook over a medium heat until lightly browned.

3 Stir in the red cabbage and cook for 5 minutes, stirring, or until the cabbage has softened slightly. Add the juniper berries, sugar, vinegar, thyme and hot stock. Season with salt and pepper.

4 Put the guinea fowl on top of the cabbage mixture, then cover the casserole tightly with a lid or double thickness of foil and braise in the oven for 1½ hours. Remove the lid and continue cooking for 30 minutes or until the birds are cooked through – the juices should run clear when you pierce the thighs with a skewer.

5 Transfer the guinea fowl to a board and spoon the cabbage and juices on to a serving platter. Keep warm. Joint the birds into eight, as you would a chicken, then arrange the guinea fowl pieces on the platter on top of the cabbage. Serve at once.

Spicy Pork & Bean Stew

Serves 4
Preparation Time
15 minutes
Cooking Time
3–4 hours on Low

Per Serving
348 calories
14g fat
(of which 3g saturates)
27g carbohydrate
1.5g salt

Gluten Free

3 tbsp olive oil
400g (14oz) pork tenderloin, cubed
1 red onion, sliced
2 leeks, trimmed and cut into chunks
2 celery sticks, trimmed and cut into chunks
½ tbsp harissa paste
1 tbsp tomato purée
1 × 400g can cherry tomatoes
150ml (5fl oz) hot vegetable or chicken stock
(see Cook's Tips, pages 69 and 17)
1 × 400g can cannellini beans, drained and rinsed
1 marinated red pepper, sliced
salt and ground black pepper
freshly chopped flat-leafed parsley to garnish
Greek-style yogurt, lemon wedges and bread
to serve

1 Heat 2 tbsp olive oil in a large pan. Add the pork and fry in batches until golden. Transfer to the slow cooker.

2 Heat the remaining oil in the pan. Add the onion and fry for 5–10 minutes until softened. Add the leek and celery and cook for 5 minutes. Add the harissa and tomato purée. Cook for 1–2 minutes, stirring all the time. Add the tomatoes and stock and season well. Bring to the boil, then pour into the slow cooker. Cover and cook on Low for 3–4 hours.

3 Stir in the drained beans and red pepper and leave to stand for 5 minutes to warm through. Garnish with parsley and serve with a dollop of Greek-style yogurt, a grinding of black pepper, lemon wedges for squeezing over the stew, and chunks of crusty baguette or wholegrain bread.

Try Something Different
Instead of pork, use the same quantity of lean lamb, such as leg, trimmed of excess fat and cut into cubes.

Without a Slow Cooker
Follow the recipe until the end of step 2, but fry the pork in a flameproof casserole. In step 2, bring to the boil, then transfer to the oven and cook for 25 minutes. Complete the recipe from step 3.

Pork & Apple Hotpot

Serves 4
Preparation Time
15 minutes
Cooking Time
2–2¼ hours

Per Serving
592 calories
18g fat
(of which 7g saturates)
56g carbohydrate
1g salt

1 tbsp olive oil
900g (2lb) pork shoulder steaks
3 onions, cut into wedges
1 large Bramley apple, peeled, cored
and thickly sliced
1 tbsp plain flour
600ml (1 pint) hot, weak vegetable
or chicken stock (see Cook's Tips,
pages 69 and 17)
¼ savoy cabbage, sliced
2 thyme sprigs
900g (2lb) large potatoes, cut into
2cm (¾in) slices
25g (1oz) butter
salt and ground black pepper

1 Preheat the oven to 170°C (150°C fan oven) mark 3. In a large non-stick flameproof casserole, heat the oil until very hot, then fry the steaks, two at a time, for 5 minutes or until golden all over. Remove the steaks from the pan and put to one side.

2 In the same casserole, fry the onions for 10 minutes or until soft – add a little water if they start to stick. Stir in the apple and cook for 1 minute, then add the flour to soak up the juices. Gradually add the hot stock and stir until smooth. Season. Stir in the cabbage and add the pork.

3 Throw in the thyme, overlap the potato slices on top, then dot with the butter. Cover with a tight-fitting lid and cook near the top of the oven for 1 hour. Remove the lid and cook for 30–45 minutes until the potatoes are tender and golden.

Freezing Tip

If you are going to freeze this dish, then use a freezerproof casserole.
To freeze Complete the recipe, cool quickly, then freeze in the casserole for up to three months.
To use Thaw overnight at cool room temperature. Preheat the oven to 180°C (160°C fan oven) mark 4. Pour 50ml (2fl oz) hot stock over the hotpot, then cover and reheat for 30 minutes or until piping hot. Uncover and crisp the potatoes under the grill for 2–3 minutes.

Cook's Tip

Put the hotpot under the grill for 2–3 minutes to crisp up the potatoes, if you like.

Belly of Pork with Cider & Rosemary

Serves 8	2kg (4½lb) piece pork belly roast, on the bone
Preparation Time	500ml bottle medium cider
30 minutes	600ml (1 pint) hot chicken stock
Cooking Time	(see Cook's Tip, page 17)
about 4½ hours, plus	6–8 fresh rosemary sprigs
cooling and chilling	3 fat garlic cloves, halved
	2 tbsp olive oil
Per serving	grated zest and juice of 1 large orange and 1 lemon
694 calories	3 tbsp light muscovado sugar
52g fat	25g (1oz) softened butter, mixed with
(of which 19g saturates)	1 tbsp plain flour (beurre manié, see Cook's Tip)
9g carbohydrates	salt and ground black pepper
0.5g salt	mixed vegetables to serve

1 Preheat the oven to 150°C (130°C fan oven) mark 2. Put the pork, skin side up, in a roasting tin just large enough to hold it. Add the cider, hot stock and half the rosemary. Bring to the boil on the hob, then cover with foil and cook in the oven for 4 hours. Leave to cool in the cooking liquid.

2 Strip the leaves from the remaining rosemary and chop. Put into a pestle and mortar with the garlic, oil, orange and lemon zest, 1 tsp salt and 1 tbsp of the sugar. Pound for 3–4 minutes to make a rough paste.

3 Remove the pork from the tin (keep the cooking liquid), slice off the rind from the top layer of fat and put to one side. Score the fat into a diamond pattern and rub in the rosemary paste. Cover loosely with clingfilm and chill until required.

4 Preheat the grill. Pat the rind dry with kitchen paper and put it fat side up on a foil-lined baking sheet. Cook under the hot grill, about 10cm (4in) away from the heat, for 5 minutes. Turn it over, sprinkle lightly with salt, then grill for 7–10 minutes until crisp. Cool, then cut the crackling into rough pieces.

5 Make the gravy. Strain the cooking liquid into a pan. Add the orange and lemon juice and the remaining 2 tbsp sugar, bring to the boil and bubble until reduced by half. Whisk the butter mixture into the liquid and boil for 4–5 minutes until thickened. Put to one side.

6 When almost ready to serve, preheat the oven to 220°C (200°C fan oven) mark 7. Cook the pork, uncovered, in a roasting tin for 20 minutes or until piping hot. Wrap the crackling in foil and warm in the oven for the last 5 minutes of the cooking time. Heat the gravy on the hob. Carve the pork into slices and serve with the crackling, gravy and vegetables.

Cook's Tip
A beurre manié is a mixture of equal parts of softened butter and flour that has been kneaded together to form a paste. It is used to thicken sauces and stews and is whisked in towards the end of cooking, then boiled briefly to allow it to thicken.

Raised Pork Pie

Serves 8

Preparation Time
45 minutes

Cooking Time
about 3½ hours,
plus cooling
and chilling

Per serving
617 calories
37g fat
(of which 14g saturates)
45g carbohydrates
2g salt

3 or 4 small veal bones
1 small onion
1 bay leaf
4 black peppercorns
900g (2lb) boneless leg or shoulder of pork, cubed
¼ tsp cayenne pepper
¼ tsp ground ginger
¼ tsp ground mace
¼ tsp dried sage
¼ tsp dried marjoram
1 tbsp salt
½ tsp pepper
150ml (¼ pint) milk and 150ml (¼ pint) water mixed
150g (5oz) lard
450g (1lb) plain flour, plus extra to dust
1 medium egg, beaten
salad to serve

1 Put the bones, onion, bay leaf and peppercorns into a pan and cover with water. Bring to the boil, then reduce the heat and simmer for 20 minutes. Boil to reduce the liquid to 150ml (¼ pint). Strain and cool. Base-line a 20.5cm (8in) springform cake tin.

2 Mix the pork with the spices and herbs, 1 tsp of the salt and the pepper.

3 Bring the milk, water and lard to the boil in a pan, then gradually beat it into the flour and remaining salt in a bowl. Knead for 3–4 minutes.

4 Roll out two-thirds of the pastry on a lightly floured surface and mould into the prepared cake tin. Cover and chill for 30 minutes. Keep the remaining pastry covered. Preheat the oven to 220°C (200°C fan oven) mark 7.

5 Spoon the meat mixture and 4 tbsp cold stock into the pastry case. Roll out the remaining pastry to make a lid and put on top of the meat mixture, sealing the pastry edges well. Decorate with pastry trimmings and make a hole in the centre. Glaze with the beaten egg.

6 Bake for 30 minutes. Cover loosely with foil, reduce the oven temperature to 180°C (160°C fan oven) mark 4 and bake for a further 2½ hours. Leave to cool.

7 Warm the remaining jellied stock until liquid, then pour into the centre hole of the pie. Chill and serve with salad.

Cook's Tip
If you have no bones available for stock, use 2 tsp gelatine to 300ml (½ pint) stock.

Ginger & Honey-glazed Ham

Serves 8–10	
Preparation Time	
1 hour	
Cooking Time	
5¾ hours	
Per Serving	
550 calories for 8	
19g fat	
(of which 6g saturates)	
48g carbohydrate	
5.5g salt	
440 calories for 10	
15g fat	
(of which 5g saturates)	
38g carbohydrate	
4.4g salt	

4.5–6.8kg (10–15lb) unsmoked gammon on the bone
2 shallots, peeled and halved
6 cloves
3 bay leaves
2 celery sticks, cut into 5cm (2in) pieces
2 tbsp English mustard
5cm (2in) piece fresh root ginger, peeled and thinly sliced

For the glaze
225g (8oz) dark brown sugar
2 tbsp clear honey

8 tbsp brandy or Madeira

For the chutney
4 mangoes, peeled, sliced and chopped into 5cm (2in) chunks
1 tsp mixed spice
4 cardamom pods, seeds removed and crushed
½ tsp ground cinnamon
4 tbsp raisins

1 Put the gammon into a large pan. Add the shallots, cloves, bay leaves, celery and cold water to cover. Bring to the boil, cover, reduce the heat and simmer gently for about 5 hours. Remove any scum with a slotted spoon. Lift the ham out of the pan, discard the vegetables and herbs, and leave to cool.

2 Preheat the oven to 200°C (180°C fan oven) mark 6. Using a sharp knife, carefully cut away the ham's thick skin to leave an even layer of fat. Score a diamond pattern in the fat and put the ham into a roasting tin. Smother evenly with the mustard and tuck the ginger into the scored fat.

3 To make the glaze, put the sugar, honey and brandy or Madeira into a pan and heat until the sugar has dissolved. Brush over the ham.

4 In a bowl, mix together the chutney ingredients, add any remaining glaze, then spoon around the ham.

5 Cook the ham for 30–40 minutes, basting every 10 minutes. Remove the ham from the roasting tin and put to one side. Stir the chutney and put it under the grill for 5 minutes to allow the mango to caramelise. Transfer the chutney to a side dish for serving.

Curried Lamb with Lentils

Serves 4
Preparation Time
15 minutes, plus
marinating
Cooking Time
20 minutes in pan
then 5-6 hours
on Low

Per Serving
478 calories
22g fat
(of which 7g saturates)
36g carbohydrate
0.3g salt

Gluten Free
Dairy Free

500g (1lb 2oz) lean stewing lamb on the
bone, cut into 8 pieces (ask your butcher
to do this), trimmed of fat
1 tsp ground cumin
1 tsp ground turmeric
2 garlic cloves, crushed
1 medium red chilli, seeded and chopped
(see Cook's Tip)
2.5cm (1in) piece fresh root ginger,
peeled and grated
2 tbsp vegetable oil
1 onion, chopped
1 × 400g can chopped tomatoes
2 tbsp vinegar
175g (6oz) red lentils, rinsed
salt and ground black pepper
fresh coriander sprigs to garnish
rocket salad to serve

1 Put the lamb into a shallow sealable container and add the spices, garlic, chilli, ginger, salt and pepper. Stir well to mix, then cover and chill in the fridge for at least 30 minutes.

2 Heat the oil in a large pan. Add the onion and cook over a low heat for 5 minutes. Add the lamb and cook for 10 minutes, turning regularly, or until the meat is evenly browned.

3 Add the tomatoes, vinegar, lentils and 225ml (8fl oz) boiling water and bring to the boil. Season well. Transfer to the slow cooker, cover and cook on Low for 5-6 hours until the lamb is tender.

4 Serve hot, garnished with coriander sprigs, with a rocket salad.

Cook's Tip
Be extremely careful when handling chillies not to touch or rub your eyes with your fingers, as they will sting. Wash knives immediately after handling chillies for the same reason. As a precaution, use rubber gloves when preparing them if you like.

Without a Slow Cooker
At the end of step 3, leave the mixture in the pan, bring to the boil, then reduce the heat, cover the pan and simmer for 1 hour. Remove the lid and cook for 30 minutes, stirring occasionally, or until the sauce is thick and the lamb is tender. Complete step 4 to serve.

Braised Lamb Shanks

Serves 6

Preparation Time

20–25 minutes

Cooking Time

2¾ hours

Per Serving

355 calories

16g fat

(of which 6g saturates)

23g carbohydrate

1.2g salt

Gluten Free Dairy Free

6 small lamb shanks
450g (1lb) shallots, peeled but left whole
2 medium aubergines, cut into small dice
2 tbsp olive oil
3 tbsp harissa paste
pared zest of 1 orange and juice of 3 large oranges
200ml (7fl oz) medium sherry
700g (1½lb) passata
300ml (½ pint) hot vegetable or lamb stock
(see Cook's Tip, pages 69)
75g (3oz) ready-to-eat dried apricots
75g (3oz) cherries (optional)
a large pinch of saffron threads
couscous and French beans (optional) to serve

1 Preheat the oven to 170°C (150°C fan oven) mark 3. Heat a large flameproof casserole over a medium heat and brown the lamb shanks all over. Allow 10–12 minutes to do this – the better the colour now, the better the flavour of the finished dish.

2 Remove the lamb and put to one side. Add the shallots, aubergines and oil to the casserole and cook over a high heat, stirring from time to time, until the shallots and aubergines are golden and beginning to soften.

3 Reduce the heat and add the lamb and all the other ingredients except the couscous and beans. The liquid should come halfway up the shanks. Bring to the boil, then cover tightly and put into the oven for 2½ hours. Test the lamb with a fork – it should be so tender that it almost falls off the bone.

4 If the cooking liquid looks too thin, remove the lamb to a heated serving plate, then bubble the sauce on the hob until reduced and thickened. Put the lamb back into the casserole. Serve with couscous and French beans, if you like.

Cook's Tip
Cooking lamb shanks in a rich sauce in the oven at a low temperature makes the meat meltingly tender.

Lamb & Barley Stew

Serves 6
Preparation Time
15 minutes
Cooking time
2½ hours

Per serving
536 calories
28g fat
(of which 12g saturates)
14g carbohydrates
1.2g salt

2 tbsp plain wholemeal flour
1.4kg (3lb) boned leg or shoulder of lamb, trimmed of fat and cubed
3 streaky bacon rashers, rind removed
25g (1oz) butter
2 medium onions, chopped
2 medium carrots, sliced
125g (4oz) turnip or swede, diced
2 celery sticks, diced
2 tbsp pearl barley
2 tsp mixed freshly chopped herbs, such as thyme, rosemary, parsley, basil
300ml (½ pint) lamb or beef stock
salt and ground black pepper
freshly chopped flat-leafed parsley to garnish

1 Season the flour with salt and pepper, then toss the lamb in the flour.

2 Dry-fry the bacon in a large flameproof casserole until the fat runs. Add the butter and the lamb and fry until browned all over, stirring. Using a slotted spoon, remove the lamb and bacon from the casserole and put to one side.

3 Add the onions, carrots, turnip or swede and celery to the casserole and fry for 5–10 minutes until beginning to brown.

4 Return the lamb to the casserole, add the pearl barley and herbs and pour in the stock. Bring to the boil, then reduce the heat, cover and simmer for 2 hours, stirring occasionally to prevent sticking, until the lamb is tender.

5 Serve hot, sprinkled with chopped parsley.

Parson's Venison

Serves 6	25g (1oz) butter
Preparation Time	1 small onion, finely chopped
10 minutes,	125g (4oz) mushrooms, chopped
plus marinating	125g (4oz) cooked ham, chopped
Cooking Time	2 tbsp snipped fresh chives
2¼–2½ hours	1.8–2kg (4–4½lb) leg of lamb, boned
Per serving	**For the marinade**
662 calories	200ml (7fl oz) dry red wine
41g fat	75ml (2½fl oz) port
(of which 19g saturates)	6 juniper berries, crushed
3g carbohydrates	¼ tsp ground allspice
1.4g salt	3 tbsp red wine vinegar
	1 bay leaf
	¼ tsp freshly grated nutmeg
	salt and ground black pepper

1 Melt half the butter in a pan. Add the onion and mushrooms and cook, stirring frequently, until the onion is soft but not browned. Stir in the ham and chives and season to taste. Leave to cool.

2 Season the lamb inside and out with pepper, then spread the onion mixture over the inside. Roll up tightly and tie securely. Put the lamb in a large glass bowl or casserole.

3 Mix all the ingredients for the marinade. Pour over the lamb, cover and leave in a cool place for 24 hours, turning occasionally.

4 The next day, preheat the oven to 180°C (160°C fan oven) mark 4. Remove the meat from the marinade, drain and dry. Reserve the marinade. Melt the remaining butter in a flameproof casserole. Add the meat and brown on all sides over a medium to high heat.

5 Pour in the marinade and bring almost to the boil, then cover and cook in the oven for 1¾–2 hours until the meat is tender, basting occasionally with marinade.

6 Transfer the meat to a warmed plate. Skim the fat from the surface of the liquid, then boil rapidly until syrupy. Remove the bay leaf, adjust the seasoning and serve with the meat.

Italian Braised Leg of Lamb

Serves 6

Preparation Time

15 minutes

Cooking Time

about 5 hours

Per Serving

400 calories

18g fat

(of which 6g saturates)

17g carbohydrate

0.7g salt

Gluten Free Dairy Free

2.3kg (5lb) boned leg of lamb
50ml (2fl oz) olive oil
700g (1½lb) onions, roughly chopped
1 each red, orange and yellow peppers,
seeded and roughly chopped
2 red chillies, seeded and finely chopped
(see Cook's Tip, page 37)
1 garlic bulb, cloves separated and peeled
3 tbsp dried oregano
75cl bottle dry white wine
3 × 400g cans cherry tomatoes
salt and ground black pepper

1 Preheat the oven to 170°C (150°C fan oven) mark 3. Season the lamb with salt and pepper. Heat 2 tbsp oil in a large deep flameproof casserole and brown the meat well. Remove and put to one side. Wipe the pan clean.

2 Heat the remaining oil in the casserole and fry the onions, peppers, chillies, garlic and oregano over a medium heat for 10–15 minutes until the onions are translucent and golden brown. Stir in the wine and tomatoes and bring to the boil. Bubble for 10 minutes.

3 Put the lamb on top of the vegetables and season. Baste the meat with the sauce and cover the casserole tightly with foil and a lid. Cook in the oven for 4 hours, basting occasionally.

4 Uncover and cook for a further 30 minutes. Serve the lamb carved into thick slices with the sauce spooned over.

Luxury Lamb & Leek Hotpot

Serves 6

Preparation Time
20 minutes

Cooking Time
2 hours 50 minutes

Per Serving
530 calories
33g fat
(of which 20g saturates)
27g carbohydrate
0.5g salt

50g (2oz) butter
400g (14oz) leeks, trimmed and sliced
1 medium onion, chopped
1 tbsp olive oil
800g (1¾lb) casserole lamb, cubed and tossed
with 1 tbsp plain flour
2 garlic cloves, crushed
800g (1¾lb) waxy potatoes, such as Desirée, sliced
3 tbsp freshly chopped flat-leafed parsley
1 tsp freshly chopped thyme
300ml (½ pint) lamb stock
142ml carton double cream
salt and ground black pepper

1 Melt half the butter in a 3.5 litre (6¼ pint) flameproof casserole. Add the leeks and onion, stir to coat, then cover and cook over a low heat for 10 minutes.

2 Transfer the leeks and onion on to a large sheet of greaseproof paper. Add the oil to the casserole and heat, then brown the meat in batches with the garlic and plenty of seasoning. Remove and put to one side on another large sheet of greaseproof paper.

3 Preheat the oven to 170°C (150°C fan oven) mark 3. Put half the potatoes in a layer over the base of the casserole and season. Add the meat, then spoon the leek mixture on top. Arrange a layer of overlapping potatoes on top of that, sprinkle with herbs, then pour in the stock.

4 Bring the casserole to the boil, then cover and transfer to a low shelf in the oven and cook for about 1 hour 50 minutes. Remove from the oven, dot with the remaining butter and add the cream. Return to the oven and cook, uncovered, for 30–40 minutes until the potatoes are golden brown.

Irish Stew

Serves 4
Preparation Time
15 minutes
Cooking Time
about 2¼ hours

Per serving
419 calories
20g fat
(of which 9g saturates)
24g carbohydrates
0.6g salt

700g (1½lb) middle neck lamb cutlets, fat trimmed
2 onions, thinly sliced
450g (1lb) potatoes, peeled and thinly sliced
1 tbsp freshly chopped flat-leafed parsley, plus extra to garnish
1 tbsp dried thyme
300ml (½ pint) lamb stock
salt and ground black pepper

1 Preheat the oven to 170°C (150°C fan oven) mark 3. Layer the meat, onions and potatoes in a deep casserole dish, sprinkling some herbs and seasoning between each layer. Finish with a layer of potato, overlapping the slices neatly.

2 Pour the stock over the potatoes, then cover with greaseproof paper and a lid. Cook for about 2 hours or until the meat is tender.

3 Preheat the grill. Take the lid off the casserole and remove the paper. Put under the grill and brown the top of the potatoes. Sprinkle with chopped parsley and serve immediately.

Braised Lamb Shanks with Cannellini Beans

Serves 6
Preparation Time
15 minutes
Cooking Time
3 hours

Per Serving
382 calories
18g fat
(of which 6g saturates)
29g carbohydrate
1.2g salt

Gluten Free
Dairy Free

3 tbsp olive oil
6 lamb shanks
1 large onion, chopped
3 carrots, sliced
3 celery sticks, trimmed and sliced
2 garlic cloves, crushed
2 × 400g cans chopped tomatoes
125ml (4fl oz) balsamic vinegar
2 bay leaves
2 × 400g cans cannellini beans,
drained and rinsed
salt and ground black pepper

1 Preheat the oven to 170°C (150°C fan oven) mark 3. Heat the oil in a large flameproof casserole and brown the lamb shanks, in two batches, all over. Remove and put to one side.

2 Add the onion, carrots, celery and garlic to the casserole and cook gently until softened and just beginning to colour.

3 Return the lamb to the casserole and add the chopped tomatoes and balsamic vinegar, giving the mixture a good stir. Season with salt and pepper and add the bay leaves. Bring to a simmer, cover and cook on the hob for 5 minutes.

4 Transfer to the oven and cook for 1½–2 hours or until the lamb shanks are nearly tender.

5 Remove the casserole from the oven and add the cannellini beans. Cover and return to the oven for a further 30 minutes, then serve.

Lamb, Potato & Peanut Curry

Serves 8

Preparation Time
20 minutes

Cooking Time
about 2 hours

Per Serving
664 calories
47g fat
(of which 20g
saturates)
19g carbohydrate
0.5g salt

Gluten Free Dairy Free

2 tbsp olive oil
1 medium onion, chopped
1 tbsp peeled and grated fresh root ginger
1.6kg (3½lb) leg of lamb, diced
3–4 tbsp Massaman paste (see Cook's Tip)
1 tbsp fish sauce
2 tbsp peanut butter
100g (3½oz) ground almonds
1 × 400ml can coconut milk
600ml (1 pint) hot chicken stock
(see Cook's Tip, page 17)
1–2 tbsp dry sherry
500g (1lb 2oz) small potatoes, peeled and
quartered
200g (7oz) green beans, trimmed
75g (3oz) toasted peanuts, roughly chopped
1 × 20g pack coriander, finely chopped
2 limes, quartered and rice to serve

1 Preheat the oven to 170°C (150°C fan oven) mark 3. Heat the oil in a large flameproof casserole. Add the onion and cook over a medium heat for 7–8 minutes until golden. Add the ginger and cook for 1 minute. Spoon the onion mixture out of the pan and put to one side. Add the lamb and fry in batches until browned. Put to one side.

2 Add the Massaman paste, fish sauce and peanut butter to the casserole and fry for 2–3 minutes, then add the reserved onion and ginger mixture, lamb pieces, the ground almonds, coconut milk, hot stock and sherry.

3 Bring to the boil, then cover with a lid and cook in the oven for 1 hour. Add the potatoes and cook for a further 40 minutes, uncovered, adding the green beans for the last 20 minutes. Garnish with toasted peanuts and coriander. Serve with freshly cooked rice and lime wedges to squeeze over the curry.

Cook's Tip

Massaman paste is a Thai curry paste. The ingredients include red chillies, roasted shallots, roasted garlic, galangal, lemongrass, roasted coriander seeds, roasted cumin, roasted cloves, white pepper, salt and shrimp paste. It's available in supermarkets or Asian food stores.

Lamb, Prune & Almond Tagine

Serves 6
Preparation Time
20 minutes, plus
marinating
Cooking Time
2½ hours

Per Serving
652 calories
44g fat
(of which 16g saturates)
31g carbohydrate
0.6g salt

Gluten Free

2 tsp coriander seeds
2 tsp cumin seeds
2 tsp chilli powder
1 tbsp paprika
1 tbsp ground turmeric
5 garlic cloves,
chopped
6 tbsp olive oil
1.4kg (3lb) lamb leg
steaks
75g (3oz) ghee or
clarified butter
(see Cook's Tip)
2 large onions, finely
chopped
1 carrot, roughly
chopped

900ml (1½ pints) lamb
stock
300g (11oz) ready-
to-eat prunes
4 cinnamon sticks
4 bay leaves
50g (2oz) ground
almonds
12 shallots
1 tbsp honey
salt and ground
black pepper
toasted blanched
almonds and freshly
chopped flat-leafed
parsley to garnish
couscous to serve

1 Using a pestle and mortar or a blender, combine the coriander and cumin seeds, chilli powder, paprika, turmeric, garlic and 4 tbsp oil. Coat the lamb with the paste, then cover and chill for at least 5 hours.

2 Preheat the oven to 170°C (150°C fan oven) mark 3. Melt 25g (1oz) ghee or butter in a large flameproof casserole. Add the onions and carrot and cook until soft. Remove and put to one side. Fry the paste-coated lamb on both sides in the remaining ghee or butter. Add a little of the stock and bring to the boil, scraping up the sediment from the bottom. Put the onions and carrot back in the casserole and add 100g (3½oz) prunes. Add the remaining stock with the cinnamon sticks, bay leaves and ground almonds. Season, cover and cook in the oven for 2 hours or until the meat is really tender.

3 Meanwhile, fry the shallots in the remaining oil and the honey until they turn a deep golden brown. Add to the casserole 30–40 minutes before the end of the cooking time.

4 Take the lamb out of the sauce and put to one side. Bring the sauce to the boil, then reduce to a thick consistency. Put the lamb back in the casserole, add the remaining prunes and bubble for 3–4 minutes. Garnish with the almonds and parsley. Serve hot with couscous.

Cook's Tip
To make clarified butter, heat butter in a pan without allowing it to colour. Skim off the foam; the solids will sink. Pour the clear butter into a bowl through a lined sieve. Leave for 10 minutes. Pour into a bowl, leaving any sediment behind. Cool. Store in a jar in the fridge for up to six months.

Beef & Stout Stew

Serves 6
Preparation Time
15 minutes
Cooking Time
8–10 hours on Low

Per serving
526 calories
29g fat
(of which 10g saturates)
10g carbohydrates
0.4g salt

1.4kg (3lb) shin of beef or braising steak, cut into 3cm (1¼in) cubes
2 tbsp seasoned plain flour
4 tbsp vegetable oil
2 medium onions, sliced
4 medium carrots, cut into chunks
225ml (8fl oz) stout
300ml (½ pint) hot beef stock
2 bay leaves
700g (1½lb) baby potatoes, halved if large
2 tbsp freshly chopped flat-leafed parsley
salt and ground black pepper

1 Toss the beef in the flour to coat and shake off any excess. Heat the oil in a large pan until hot. Add a handful of beef and cook until well browned. Remove with a slotted spoon, transfer to the slow cooker and repeat until all the meat is browned.

2 Add the onions and carrots to the pan and cook for 10 minutes or until browned. Add the stout, scraping the base of the pan to loosen the sediment, then stir in the hot stock. Add the bay leaves and baby potatoes and bring to the boil. Pour over the beef in the slow cooker, then cover and cook on Low for 8–10 hours until the meat is tender.

3 Stir in the parsley, season to taste and serve.

Pheasant Casserole with Cider & Apples

Serves 8
Preparation Time
50 minutes
Cooking Time
40 minutes in pan
and 6–7 hours
on Low

Per Serving
478 calories
28g fat
(of which 16g saturates)
12g carbohydrate
0.7g salt

2 large, oven-ready pheasants
2 tbsp plain flour, plus extra to dust
50g (2oz) butter
4 rindless streaky bacon rashers, halved
2 onions, chopped
2 celery sticks, trimmed and chopped
1 tbsp dried juniper berries, lightly crushed
2.5cm (1in) piece fresh root ginger, peeled
and finely chopped
150ml (¼ pint) hot pheasant or chicken stock
(see Cook's Tip, page 17)
350ml (12fl oz) dry cider
150ml (¼ pint) double cream
4 crisp eating apples, such as Granny Smith
1 tbsp lemon juice
salt and ground black pepper

1 Cut each pheasant into four portions, season with salt and pepper and dust with flour.

2 Melt three-quarters of the butter in a large pan and brown the pheasant portions, in batches, over a high heat until deep golden brown on all sides. Transfer to the slow cooker.

3 Add the bacon to the pan and fry for 2–3 minutes until golden. Add the onions, celery, juniper and ginger and cook for 8–10 minutes.

4 Stir in the flour and cook, stirring, for 2 minutes, then add the hot stock and the cider and bring to the boil, stirring. Pour into the slow cooker and season well, then cover and cook on Low for 6–7 hours or until the pheasant is tender.

5 Lift out the pheasant and put into a warmed dish and keep it warm. Strain the sauce through a sieve into a pan. Stir in the cream, bring to the boil and bubble for 10 minutes or until syrupy.

6 Quarter, core and cut the apples into wedges, then toss in the lemon juice. Melt the remaining butter in a small pan and fry the apple wedges for 2–3 minutes until golden. Return the pheasant to the sauce, along with the apples, and check the seasoning before serving.

Braised Beef with Pancetta & Mushrooms

Serves 4
Preparation Time
20 minutes
Cooking Time
about 3½ hours

Per Serving
541 calories
25g fat
(of which 9g saturates)
30g carbohydrate
1.6g salt

Dairy Free

175g (6oz) smoked pancetta
or smoked streaky bacon, cubed
2 leeks, trimmed and thickly sliced
1 tbsp olive oil
450g (1lb) braising steak, cut into
5cm (2in) pieces
1 large onion, finely chopped
2 carrots, thickly sliced
2 parsnips, thickly sliced
1 tbsp plain flour
300ml (½ pint) red wine
1–2 tbsp redcurrant jelly
125g (4oz) chestnut mushrooms, halved
ground black pepper
freshly chopped flat-leafed parsley to garnish

1 Preheat the oven to 170°C (150°C fan oven) mark 3. Fry the pancetta or bacon in a shallow flameproof casserole for 2–3 minutes until golden. Add the leeks and cook for a further 2 minutes or until they are just beginning to colour. Remove with a slotted spoon and put to one side.

2 Heat the oil in the casserole. Fry the beef in batches for 2–3 minutes until golden brown on all sides. Remove and put to one side. Add the onion and fry over a gentle heat for 5 minutes or until golden. Stir in the carrots and parsnips and fry for 1–2 minutes.

3 Put the beef back into the casserole and stir in the flour to soak up the juices. Gradually add the wine and 300ml (½ pint) water, then stir in the redcurrant jelly. Season with pepper and bring to the boil. Cover with a tight-fitting lid and cook in the oven for 2 hours.

4 Stir in the leeks, pancetta and mushrooms, cover and cook for a further 1 hour or until everything is tender. Serve hot, sprinkled with chopped parsley.

Freezing Tip
To freeze Complete the recipe to the end of step 4, without the garnish. Put into a freezerproof container, cool and freeze for up to three months.
To use Thaw overnight at cool room temperature. Preheat the oven to 180°C (160°C fan oven) mark 4. Bring to the boil on the hob, cover tightly and reheat in the oven for about 30 minutes or until piping hot.

Beef Casserole with Black Olives

Serves 6	6 tbsp oil
Preparation Time	1.1kg (2½lb) stewing steak, cut
20 minutes	into 4cm (1½in) cubes
Cooking Time	350g (12oz) unsmoked streaky bacon rashers,
2 hours 10 minutes	rind removed and sliced into thin strips
	450g (1lb) onions, roughly chopped
Per Serving	3 large garlic cloves
704 calories	2 tbsp tomato purée
45g fat	125ml (4fl oz) brandy
(of which 13g saturates)	1 tbsp plain flour
9g carbohydrate	150ml (¼ pint) red wine
3.3g salt	300ml (½ pint) beef stock
	1 bouquet garni (see Cook's Tip, page 73)
Dairy Free	225g (8oz) flat mushrooms, quartered if large
	125g (4oz) black olives
	fresh flat-leafed parsley sprigs to garnish (optional)

1 Heat 3 tbsp oil in a large flameproof casserole over a high heat. Brown the steak in batches until dark chestnut brown, then remove from the pan and keep warm. Add the bacon and fry until golden brown, then put to one side with the beef.

2 Add the remaining oil and cook the onions over a medium heat for 10–15 minutes until golden. Add the garlic, fry for 30 seconds, then add the tomato purée and cook, stirring, for 1–2 minutes. Add the brandy.

3 Preheat the oven to 170°C (150°C fan oven) mark 3. Bring the casserole to the boil and bubble to reduce by half, then add the flour and mix until smooth. Pour in the wine, bring back to the boil and bubble for 1 minute. Put the steak and bacon back into the casserole, then add enough stock to barely cover the meat. Add the bouquet garni. Bring to the boil, then cover, put into the oven and cook for 1¼–1½ hours until the steak is tender. Add the mushrooms and cook for a further 4–5 minutes.

4 Just before serving, remove the bouquet garni and stir in the black olives. Serve hot, garnished with parsley, if you like.

Freezing Tip
To freeze Complete the recipe to the end of step 3. Cool quickly and put into a freezerproof container. Seal and freeze for up to one month.
To use Thaw overnight at cool room temperature. Preheat the oven to 180°C (160°C fan oven) mark 4. Bring slowly to the boil on the hob, then cover and reheat in the oven for 20–25 minutes. Complete the recipe.

Beef Goulash

Serves 6	1kg (2¼lb) stewing steak
Preparation Time	2 tbsp seasoned plain flour
30 minutes	3 tbsp vegetable oil
Cooking Time	700g (1½lb) onions, chopped
20 minutes in pan	225g (8oz) pancetta cubes or bacon lardons
then 8–10 hours	2 garlic cloves, crushed
on Low	4 tbsp paprika
	2 tsp dried mixed herbs
Per Serving	1 × 400g can peeled plum tomatoes
726 calories	150ml (¼ pint) hot beef stock
44g fat	150ml (¼ pint) soured cream
(of which 16g saturates)	salt and ground black pepper
21g carbohydrate	freshly chopped parsley to garnish
1.6g salt	noodles to serve

1 Cut the beef into 3cm (1¼in) cubes, then toss the cubes in the flour to coat and shake off any excess.

2 Heat 2 tbsp oil in a large pan and quickly fry the meat in small batches until browned on all sides. Transfer to the slow cooker.

3 Heat the remaining oil in the pan, add the onions and fry gently for 5–7 minutes until starting to soften and turn golden. Add the pancetta or lardons and fry over a high heat until crispy. Stir in the garlic and paprika and cook, stirring, for 1 minute.

4 Add the herbs, tomatoes and hot stock and bring to the boil. Stir into the beef in the slow cooker, cover and cook on Low for 8–10 hours until tender.

5 Check the seasoning, then stir in the soured cream. Garnish with parsley and serve with noodles.

Without a Slow Cooker

Cook the recipe in a deep, flameproof casserole. Preheat the oven to 170°C (fan oven 150°C) mark 3. At the end of step 2, transfer the meat to a plate, then return it to the casserole at the end of step 3. Add the ingredients described in step 4, then bring to a simmer, cover tightly and cook in the oven for 1½ hours, topping up the liquid after 1 hour if necessary. Complete step 5 to finish the recipe.

Smoky Pimento Goulash

Serves 8	
Preparation Time	
20 minutes	
Cooking Time	
about 3 hours	
Per Serving	
515 calories	
35g fat	
(of which 14g saturates)	
13g carbohydrates	
1.3g salt	

1.1kg (2½lb)
braising steak
3 tbsp olive oil
16 shallots or
button onions
225g (8oz) piece
chorizo sausage,
roughly chopped
1 red chilli, seeded
and chopped (see
Cook's Tip, page 37)
3 bay leaves
3 garlic cloves,
crushed
2 tbsp plain flour
2 tbsp smoked paprika
700g jar passata
100ml (3½fl oz)

hot beef stock
salt and ground
black pepper
mashed potatoes (see
Cook's Tip, page 63)
and green vegetables
to serve

**For the minted
soured cream**
284ml carton
soured cream
1 tbsp finely chopped
fresh mint
1 tbsp extra virgin
olive oil, plus extra
to drizzle

1 Mix together all the ingredients for the minted soured cream and season with a little salt and plenty of coarsely ground black pepper. Cover and chill in the fridge until needed.

2 Preheat the oven to 170°C (150°C fan oven) mark 3. Cut the braising steak into large cubes, slightly larger than bite-size.

3 Heat the olive oil in a 4 litre (7 pint) flameproof casserole until really hot. Brown the beef, a few cubes at a time, over a high heat until it is deep brown all over. Remove with a slotted spoon and put to one side. Repeat with the remaining beef until all the pieces have been browned.

4 Reduce the heat under the casserole, then add the shallots, chorizo, chilli, bay leaves and garlic. Fry for 7–10 minutes until the shallots are golden brown and beginning to soften. Return the meat to the casserole and stir in the flour and paprika. Cook, stirring, for 1–2 minutes, then add the passata. Season, cover and cook in the oven for 2½ hours or until the beef is meltingly tender. Check halfway through cooking – if the beef looks dry, add the hot stock. Serve with the minted soured cream, drizzled with a little olive oil and a grinding of black pepper, and some creamy mashed potatoes and green vegetables.

Get Ahead

To prepare ahead Complete the recipe. Cool and chill (it will keep for up to three days) or freeze (it will keep for up to one month).
To use, if frozen Thaw overnight at a cool room temperature. Return the goulash to the casserole, bring to the boil, reduce the heat and simmer gently for 15–20 minutes until piping hot, adding 100ml (3½fl oz) hot beef stock if it looks dry.

Braised Oxtail

Serves 6

Preparation Time
20 minutes

Cooking Time
about 4 hours

Per Serving
616 calories
35g fat
(of which 12g saturates)
16g carbohydrates
1.2g salt

2 oxtails, about 1.6kg (3½lb) in total, trimmed
2 tbsp plain flour
4 tbsp oil
2 large onions, sliced
900ml (1½ pints) beef stock
150ml (¼ pint) red wine
1 tbsp tomato purée
finely grated zest of ½ lemon
2 bay leaves
2 medium carrots, chopped
450g (1lb) parsnips, chopped
salt and ground black pepper
freshly chopped flat-leafed parsley to garnish

1 Cut the oxtails into large pieces. Season the flour with salt and pepper and use to coat the pieces. Heat the oil in a large flameproof casserole and brown the oxtail pieces, a few at a time. Remove from the casserole with a slotted spoon and put to one side.

2 Add the onions to the casserole and fry over a medium heat for about 10 minutes or until softened and lightly browned. Stir in any remaining flour.

3 Stir in the stock, red wine, tomato purée, lemon zest and bay leaves. Season with salt and pepper. Bring to the boil, then return the oxtail to the casserole and reduce the heat. Cover and simmer very gently for 2 hours.

4 Skim off the fat from the surface, then stir in the carrots and parsnips. Re-cover the casserole and simmer very gently for a further 2 hours or until the oxtail is very tender.

5 Skim off all the fat from the surface, then check the seasoning. Serve scattered with chopped parsley.

Cook's Tip

Oxtail contains a modest amount of meat and often plenty of firm white fat, although the fat can be trimmed before cooking. It also releases generous amounts of gelatine, which helps to enrich dishes.

Mexican Chilli con Carne

Serves 4
Preparation Time
5 minutes
Cooking Time
25 minutes in pan
then 4–5 hours
on Low

Per Serving
408 calories
19g fat
(of which 7g saturates)
28g carbohydrate
1.1g salt

Gluten Free
Dairy Free

2 tbsp olive oil
450g (1lb) minced beef
1 large onion, finely chopped
½–1 tsp each hot chilli powder and ground cumin
3 tbsp tomato purée
150ml (¼ pint) hot beef stock
1 × 400g can chopped tomatoes with garlic
(see Cook's Tips)
25g (1oz) plain chocolate
1 × 400g can red kidney beans, drained and rinsed
2 × 20g packs coriander, chopped
salt and ground black pepper
guacamole, salsa, soured cream, grated cheese,
tortilla chips and pickled chillies to serve

1 Heat 1 tbsp oil in a large pan and fry the beef for 10 minutes or until well browned, stirring to break up any lumps. Remove from the pan with a slotted spoon and transfer to the slow cooker.

2 Add the remaining oil to the pan, then fry the onion, stirring, for 10 minutes or until soft and golden.

3 Add the spices and fry for 1 minute, then add the tomato purée, hot stock and the tomatoes. Bring to the boil, then stir into the mince in the slow cooker. Cover and cook on Low for 4–5 hours.

4 Stir in the chocolate, kidney beans and coriander and season with salt and pepper, then leave to stand for 10 minutes.

5 Serve with guacamole, salsa, soured cream, grated cheese, tortilla chips and pickled chillies.

Cook's Tips
Instead of a can of tomatoes with garlic, use a can of chopped tomatoes and 1 crushed garlic clove.
Adding a little dark chocolate to chilli con carne brings out the flavours of this tasty dish.

Without a Slow Cooker
Follow step 1, then transfer the beef to a plate and complete step 2. At the end of step 3, leave the mixture in the pan, return the beef to the pan and simmer, uncovered, for 35–40 minutes until thickened. Stir in the ingredients as described in step 4 and simmer for 5 minutes. Serve as described.

Steak & Onion Puff Pie

Serves 4

Preparation Time
30 minutes

Cooking Time
about 2½ hours

Per Serving
1036 calories
67g fat
(of which 10g saturates)
65g carbohydrate
1.4g salt

3 tbsp vegetable oil
2 onions, sliced
900g (2lb) casserole beef, cut into chunks
3 tbsp plain flour, plus extra to dust
500ml (18fl oz) hot beef stock
2 fresh rosemary sprigs, bruised
1 × 500g pack puff pastry
1 medium egg, beaten, to glaze
salt and ground black pepper

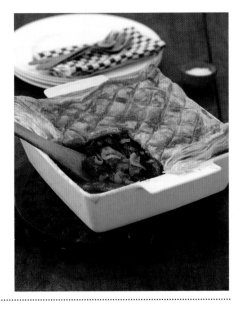

1 Preheat the oven to 170°C (150°C fan oven) mark 3.

2 Heat 1 tbsp oil in a large flameproof casserole. Add the onions and sauté for 10 minutes or until golden. Lift out and put to one side. Sear the meat in the same casserole, in batches, using more oil as necessary, until brown all over. Lift out each batch as soon as it is browned and put to one side. Add the flour to the casserole and cook for 1–2 minutes to brown. Return the onions and beef to the casserole and add the hot stock and the rosemary. Season well with salt and pepper. Cover and bring to the boil, then cook in the oven for 1½ hours or until the meat is tender.

3 About 30 minutes before the end of the cooking time, lightly dust a worksurface with flour and roll out the pastry. Cut out a lid using a 1.1 litre (2 pint) pie dish as a template, or use four 300ml (½ pint) dishes and cut out four lids. Put on a baking sheet and chill.

4 Remove the casserole from the oven. Increase the heat to 220°C (200°C fan oven) mark 7. Pour the casserole into the pie dish (or dishes), brush the edge with water and put on the pastry lid. Press lightly to seal. Lightly score the top and brush with the egg. Put the dish back on the baking sheet. Bake for 30 minutes or until the pastry is risen and golden. Serve immediately.

Freezing Tip

To freeze Complete the recipe to the end of step 3. Cool the casserole quickly. Put the beef mixture into a pie dish. Brush the dish edge with water, put on the pastry and press down lightly to seal. Score the pastry. Cover with clingfilm and freeze for up to three months.

To use Thaw overnight at cool room temperature or in the fridge. Lightly score the pastry, brush with beaten egg and cook at 220°C (200°C fan oven) mark 7 for 35 minutes or until the pastry is brown and the filling piping hot.

Braised Beef with Mustard & Capers

Serves 4
Preparation Time
15 minutes
Cooking Time
2 hours 20 minutes,
plus cooling

Per Serving
391 calories
19g fat
(of which 7g saturates)
10g carbohydrate
1.5g salt

Gluten Free
Dairy Free

50g (2oz) can anchovy fillets in oil, drained,
chopped and oil put to one side
olive oil
700g (1½lb) braising steak,
cut into small strips
2 large Spanish onions, thinly sliced
2 tbsp capers
1 tsp English mustard
6 fresh thyme sprigs
20g pack flat-leafed parsley, roughly chopped
salt and ground black pepper
green salad and crusty bread
or mashed potato (see Cook's Tip) to serve

1 Preheat the oven to 170°C (150°C fan oven) mark 3. Measure the anchovy oil into a deep flameproof casserole, then make up to 3 tbsp with the olive oil. Heat the oil and fry the meat, a few pieces at a time, until well browned. Remove with a slotted spoon and put to one side. When all the meat has been browned, pour 4 tbsp cold water into the empty casserole and stir to loosen any bits on the bottom.

2 Put the meat back into the pan and add the onions, anchovies, capers, mustard, half the thyme and all but 1 tbsp of the parsley. Stir until thoroughly mixed.

3 Tear off a sheet of greaseproof paper big enough to cover the pan. Crumple it up and wet it under the cold tap. Squeeze out most of the water, open it out and press down over the surface of the meat.

4 Cover with a tight-fitting lid and cook in the oven for 2 hours or until the beef is meltingly tender. Check the casserole after 1 hour to make sure it's still moist. If it looks dry, add a little water.

5 Adjust for seasoning, then stir in the remaining parsley and thyme. Serve with a green salad and crusty bread or mashed potato.

Cook's Tip
To make a deliciously easy mash, put four baking potatoes into the oven when you put in the casserole. Leave to bake for 2 hours. Cut each potato in half and use a fork to scrape out the flesh into a bowl. Add 50g (2oz) butter and season well with salt and pepper – the potato will be soft enough to mash with the fork.

Braised Beef with Chestnuts & Celery

Serves 6
Preparation Time
25 minutes
Cooking Time
2 hours 20 minutes

Per serving
336 calories
16g fat
(of which 6g saturates)
12g carbohydrates
1.3g salt

18 fresh chestnuts, skins split
15g (½oz) butter
1 tbsp vegetable oil
2 bacon rashers, rind removed, chopped
900g (2lb) stewing steak, cubed
1 medium onion, chopped
1 tbsp plain flour
300ml (½ pint) brown ale
300ml (½ pint) beef stock
a pinch of freshly grated nutmeg
finely grated zest and juice of 1 orange
3 celery sticks, chopped
salt and ground black pepper
freshly chopped flat-leafed parsley to garnish

1 Preheat the oven to 170°C (150°C fan oven) mark 3. Cook the chestnuts in simmering water for about 7 minutes. Remove from the water one at a time and peel off the thick outer skin and thin inner skin while still warm.

2 Heat the butter and oil in a flameproof casserole. Add the bacon and beef in batches and cook, stirring occasionally, until browned. Remove the meat with a slotted spoon.

3 Add the onion to the casserole and fry, stirring, until softened. Drain off most of the fat. Return the meat to the casserole, sprinkle in the flour and cook, stirring, for 1–2 minutes.

4 Stir in the brown ale, stock, nutmeg, orange juice and half the zest. Season to taste. Bring to the boil, stir well to loosen the sediment, then add the chestnuts. Cover tightly with foil and a lid and cook in the oven for about 45 minutes.

5 After 45 minutes, add the celery to the casserole and cook for a further 1 hour or until the meat is tender. Serve with the remaining orange zest and the parsley sprinkled over the top.

Cook's Tip
It's well worth spending the extra time needed to shell the chestnuts, as they do add a very special flavour to the finished dish.

Peppered Winter Stew

Serves 6
Preparation Time
20 minutes
Cooking Time
2¾ hours

Per Serving
540 calories
24g fat
(of which 7g saturates)
24g carbohydrate
1.5g salt

Dairy Free

25g (1oz) plain flour
900g (2lb) stewing
venison, beef or lamb,
cut into 4cm (1½in)
cubes
5 tbsp oil
225g (8oz) button
onions or shallots,
peeled with root intact
225g (8oz) onion,
finely chopped
4 garlic cloves, crushed
2 tbsp tomato purée
125ml (4fl oz) red wine
vinegar
1 × 750ml bottle red wine
2 tbsp redcurrant jelly

small bunch of thyme,
plus extra sprigs to
garnish (optional)
4 bay leaves
6 cloves
900g (2lb) mixed root
vegetables, such as
carrots, parsnips,
turnips and celeriac,
cut into 4cm (1½in)
chunks; carrots cut
a little smaller
600–900ml (1–1½ pints)
beef stock
salt and ground black
pepper

1 Preheat the oven to 180°C (160°C fan oven) mark 4. Put the flour into a plastic bag, season with salt and pepper, then toss the meat in it.

2 Heat 3 tbsp oil in a large flameproof casserole over a medium heat and brown the meat well in small batches. Remove and put to one side.

3 Heat the remaining oil and fry the button onions or shallots for 5 minutes or until golden. Add the chopped onion and the garlic and cook, stirring, until soft and golden. Add the tomato purée and cook for a further 2 minutes, then add the vinegar and wine and bring to the boil. Bubble for 10 minutes.

4 Add the redcurrant jelly, thyme, bay leaves, 1 tbsp coarsely ground black pepper, the cloves and meat to the pan, with the vegetables and enough stock to barely cover the meat and vegetables. Bring to the boil, then reduce the heat, cover the pan and cook in the oven for 1¾–2¼ hours until the meat is very tender. Serve hot, garnished with thyme sprigs, if you like.

Freezing Tip

To freeze Complete the recipe to the end of step 4, without the garnish. Cool quickly and put in a freezerproof container. Seal and freeze for up to one month.
To use Thaw overnight at cool room temperature. Preheat the oven to 180°C (160°C fan oven) mark 4. Put into a flameproof casserole and add an extra 150ml (¼ pint) beef stock. Bring to the boil. Cover and reheat for 30 minutes.

Beef with Beer & Mushrooms

Serves 4	700g (1½lb) braising steak, cut into large chunks
Preparation Time	about 5cm (2in) across
15 minutes	2 tsp plain gluten-free flour
Cooking Time	2 tbsp oil
2¾–3 hours	25g (1oz) butter
	2 large onions, finely sliced
Per Serving	225g (8oz) carrots, cut into large sticks
450 calories	200ml (7fl oz) Guinness
22g fat	300ml (½ pint) vegetable stock
(of which 8g saturates)	(see Cook's Tip, page 69)
21g carbohydrate	2 tsp tomato purée
0.6g salt	2 tsp English mustard
	2 tsp light muscovado sugar
Gluten Free	225g (8oz) large field mushrooms
Dairy Free	salt and ground black pepper
	mashed potatoes (see Cook's Tip, page 63) and
	rocket leaves to serve

1 Preheat the oven to 150°C (130°C fan oven) mark 2. Toss the meat in the flour. Heat the oil and butter in a large flameproof casserole over a medium heat and sear the meat, a few pieces at a time, until brown all over. Lift out each batch as soon as it is browned and put to one side. The flavour and colour of the finished casserole depend on the meat taking on a good deep colour now. Stir the onions into the casserole and cook for about 10 minutes.

2 Return all the meat to the casserole, add the carrots, then stir in the Guinness, stock, tomato purée, mustard, sugar and plenty of seasoning. Bring to the boil and stir well, then cover tightly with foil or a lid and simmer gently in the oven for 1½ hours.

3 Stir the whole mushrooms into the casserole and return to the oven for a further 45 minutes–1 hour until the meat is meltingly tender. Serve with mashed potatoes and rocket leaves.

Carrot & Coriander Soup

Serves 6	40g (1½oz) butter
Preparation Time	175g (6oz) leeks, trimmed and sliced
15 minutes	450g (1lb) carrots, sliced
Cooking Time	2 tsp ground coriander
15 minutes in pan	1 tsp plain flour
then 3–4 hours	1 litre (1¾ pints) hot vegetable stock
on High	(see Cook's Tip)
	150ml (¼ pint) single cream
Per Serving	salt and ground black pepper
140 calories	fresh coriander leaves, roughly torn, to serve
11g fat	
(of which 7g saturates)	
10g carbohydrate	
0.2g salt	
Vegetarian	
Gluten Free	

1 Melt the butter in a large pan. Add the leeks and carrots, stir, then cover the pan and cook gently for 7–10 minutes until the vegetables begin to soften but not colour.

2 Stir in the ground coriander and flour and cook, stirring, for 1 minute.

3 Add the hot stock and bring to the boil, stirring. Season with salt and pepper, then transfer to the slow cooker and cook on High for 3–4 hours until the vegetables are tender.

4 Leave the soup to cool a little, then whiz in batches in a blender or food processor until quite smooth. Pour into a clean pan and stir in the cream. Adjust the seasoning and reheat gently on the hob; do not boil. Ladle into warmed bowls, scatter with torn coriander leaves and serve.

Cook's Tip

Vegetable Stock Put 225g (8oz) roughly chopped onions, 225g (8oz) roughly chopped celery sticks, 225g (8oz) trimmed and roughly chopped leeks and 225g (8oz) roughly chopped carrots into a large pan. Add 1.7 litres (3 pints) cold water, 2 bay leaves, a few fresh thyme sprigs, 1 small bunch of parsley, 10 black peppercorns and ½ tsp sea salt then bring slowly to the boil and skim the surface. Partially cover the pan, then reduce the heat and simmer for 30 minutes; check the seasoning. Strain the stock through a fine sieve into a bowl and leave to cool. Cover and keep in the fridge for up to three days. Use as required. Makes 1.1 litres (2 pints).

Without a Slow Cooker

In step 3, bring to the boil and leave the soup in the pan. Season with salt and pepper, then reduce the heat, cover the pan and simmer for about 20 minutes until the vegetables are tender. Complete the recipe as directed from step 4.

Beetroot Soup

Serves 8	750g (1lb 10oz) raw beetroot
Preparation Time	1 tbsp olive oil
15 minutes	1 onion, finely chopped
Cooking Time	275g (10oz) potatoes, peeled and roughly chopped
15 minutes in pan	1.5 litres (2½ pints) hot vegetable stock
then 3–4 hours	(see Cook's Tip, page 69)
on High	juice of 1 lemon
	salt and ground black pepper

Per Serving
290 calories
25g fat
(of which 4g saturates)
15g carbohydrate
0.2g salt

To serve
125ml (4fl oz) soured cream
25g (1oz) mixed root vegetable crisps (optional)
2 tbsp snipped fresh chives

Vegetarian
Gluten Free

1 Peel the beetroot and cut into 1cm (½in) cubes. Heat the oil in a large pan. Add the onion and cook for 5 minutes to soften. Add the beetroot and potatoes and cook for a further 5 minutes.

2 Add the stock and lemon juice, and bring to the boil. Season with salt and pepper, transfer to the slow cooker and cook on High for 3–4 hours until the beetroot is tender. Cool slightly, then whiz in a blender or food processor until smooth.

3 Pour the soup into a clean pan and reheat gently on the hob. Divide the soup among warmed bowls. Swirl 1 tbsp soured cream on each portion, scatter with a few vegetable crisps if you like, and sprinkle with snipped chives to serve.

Without a Slow Cooker
In step 2, after bringing to the boil, leave the mixture in the pan, reduce the heat and simmer gently, half-covered, for 25 minutes. Leave to cool a little, then whiz in a blender or food processor until smooth. Complete the recipe as directed from step 3.

Freezing Tip
To freeze Complete the recipe to the end of step 2, then cool half or all the soup, pack and freeze for up to three months.
To use Thaw the soup overnight and simmer over a low heat for 5 minutes.

French Onion Soup

Serves 4

Preparation Time
30 minutes

Cooking Time
40 minutes in pan
then 3–4 hours
on Low

Per Serving
438 calories
21.2g fat
(of which 13.2g saturates)
45.4g carbohydrate
1.3g salt

Vegetarian

75g (3oz) butter
700g (1½lb) onions, sliced
3 garlic cloves, crushed
1 tbsp plain flour
200ml (7fl oz) dry white wine
1 litre (1¾ pints) hot vegetable stock
(see Cook's Tip, page 69)
bouquet garni (see Cook's Tip)
salt and ground black pepper
1 small baguette, cut into slices
1cm (½in) thick
50g (2oz) Gruyère cheese or Cheddar,
grated, to serve

1 Melt the butter in a large pan. Add the onions and cook slowly over a very low heat, stirring frequently, until very soft and golden brown; this should take at least 30 minutes. Add the garlic and flour and cook, stirring, for 1 minute.

2 Pour in the wine and let bubble until reduced by half. Add the stock, bouquet garni and seasoning. Bring to the boil, transfer to the slow cooker, cover and cook on Low for 3–4 hours until the onions are meltingly tender.

3 Preheat the grill. Lightly toast the slices of baguette on both sides. Reheat the soup and adjust the seasoning. Discard the bouquet garni.

4 Divide the soup among four ovenproof soup bowls. Float two or three slices of toast on each portion and sprinkle thickly with the grated cheese. Stand the bowls under a hot grill until the cheese has melted and turned golden brown. Serve at once.

Cook's Tip
To make a bouquet garni, tie together a sprig each of thyme and parsley with a bay leaf and a piece of celery.

Without a Slow Cooker
In step 2, bring to the boil, then reduce the heat and simmer gently, uncovered, for 20–30 minutes. Complete the recipe as directed from step 3.

Scotch Broth

Serves 8

Preparation Time
15 minutes

Cooking Time
15 minutes in pan
then 8–10 hours
on Low

Per Serving
173 calories
2g fat
(of which trace saturates)
35g carbohydrate
2.3g salt

Dairy Free

1.4kg (3lb) piece beef skirt
(ask your butcher for this)
300g (11oz) broth mix
(to include pearl barley, red lentils, split
peas and green peas), soaked according
to the pack instructions
2 carrots, finely chopped
1 parsnip, finely chopped
2 onions, finely chopped
¼ white cabbage, finely chopped
1 leek, trimmed and finely chopped
1 piece marrow bone, about 350g (12oz)
½ tbsp salt
ground black pepper
2 tbsp freshly chopped parsley to garnish

1 Put the beef into a large pan and cover with water. Slowly bring to the boil, then reduce the heat and simmer for 10 minutes, using a slotted spoon to remove any scum that comes to the surface. Drain.

2 Put the broth mix and all the vegetables into the slow cooker, then place the beef and marrow bone on top. Add 1.5 litres (2½ pints) boiling water – there should be enough to just cover the meat. Cover and cook on Low for 8–10 hours until the meat is tender.

3 Remove the marrow bone and beef from the broth. Add a few shreds of beef to the broth, if you like. Season the broth well with the salt and some pepper, stir in the chopped parsley and serve hot.

Cook's Tip
This can be two meals in one: a starter and a main course. The beef flavours the stock and is removed before serving. You can then divide up the meat and serve it with mashed potatoes, swedes or turnips.

Without a Slow Cooker
Follow step 1, also adding the marrow bone to the pan along with the beef. At the end of the step, do not drain but instead add the broth mix and simmer, partially covered, for 1½ hours, skimming occasionally. Add the vegetables and 600ml (1 pint) cold water and bring to the boil, then reduce the heat and summer for 30 minutes. Complete the recipe as directed from step 3.

Leek & Potato Soup

Serves 4

Preparation Time
10 minutes

Cooking Time
30 minutes in pan
then 3-4 hours
on Low

Per Serving
117 calories
6g fat
(of which 4g saturates)
13g carbohydrate
0.1g salt

Vegetarian
Gluten Free

25g (1oz) butter
1 onion, finely chopped
1 garlic clove, crushed
550g (1¼lb) leeks, trimmed and chopped
200g (7oz) floury potatoes, peeled and sliced
1.2 litres (2 pints) hot vegetable stock
(see Cook's Tip, page 69)
crème fraîche and chopped chives to garnish

1 Melt the butter in a pan over a gentle heat. Add the onion and cook for 10-15 minutes until soft. Add the garlic and cook for a further 1 minute. Add the leeks and cook for 5-10 minutes until softened. Add the potatoes and toss together with the leeks.

2 Pour in the hot stock and bring to the boil. Transfer the soup to the slow cooker, cover and cook on Low for 3-4 hours until the potatoes are tender.

3 Leave to cool a little, then whiz in batches in a blender or food processor until smooth.

4 Reheat before serving, garnished with crème fraîche and chives.

Without a Slow Cooker
In step 2, bring to the boil, then reduce the heat and simmer for 20 minutes until the potatoes are tender. Complete the recipe as directed from step 3.

Goulash Soup

Serves 6

Preparation Time

20 minutes

Cooking Time

2¾ hours

Per Serving

594 calories

30g fat

(of which 15g saturates)

35.5g carbohydrate

1.9g salt

Gluten Free

700g (1½lb) silverside or lean chuck steak
25g (1oz) butter
225g (8oz) onions, chopped
1 small green pepper, seeded and chopped
4 tomatoes, skinned and quartered
150g (5oz) tomato purée
600ml (1 pint) rich beef stock
1 tbsp paprika
450g (1lb) potatoes, peeled
150ml (¼ pint) soured cream
salt and ground black pepper
freshly chopped parsley to garnish (optional)

1 Wipe the meat with a damp cloth. Remove any excess fat or gristle and cut the meat into small pieces. Season well with 2 tsp salt and pepper to taste.

2 Melt the butter in a large pan. Add the onions and green pepper and sauté until tender.

3 Add the meat pieces, tomatoes, tomato purée, stock and paprika. Stir well and bring to the boil, then reduce the heat, cover the pan and simmer for 2½ hours, stirring occasionally.

4 Half an hour before the end of cooking, cut the potatoes into bite-size pieces, bring to the boil in lightly salted water, then reduce the heat and simmer until cooked. Drain well and add to the soup.

5 Check the seasoning and stir in 2 tbsp soured cream. Ladle into warmed bowls, garnish with chopped parsley, if you like, and serve the remaining soured cream separately, for each person to spoon into their soup.

Split Pea & Ham Soup

Serves 6	1 × 500g pack dried yellow split peas, soaked
Preparation Time	overnight (see Cook's Tip)
15 minutes, plus	25g (1oz) butter
overnight soaking	1 large onion, finely chopped
Cooking Time	125g (4oz) rindless smoked streaky bacon rashers,
15 minutes in pan	roughly chopped
then 3–4 hours	1 garlic clove, crushed
on High	1.7 litres (3 pints) well-flavoured ham or vegetable
	stock (see Cook's Tip, page 69)
Per Serving	1 bouquet garni (see Cook's Tip, page 73)
400 calories	1 tsp dried oregano
10g fat	125g (4oz) cooked ham, chopped
(of which 5g saturates)	salt and ground black pepper
53g carbohydrate	cracked black pepper to serve
1.5g salt	
Gluten Free	

1 Drain the soaked split peas. Melt the butter in a large pan. Add the onion, bacon and garlic and cook over a low heat for about 10 minutes or until the onion is soft.

2 Add the drained split peas to the pan with the stock. Bring to the boil and use a slotted spoon to remove any scum that comes to the surface. Add the bouquet garni and oregano, then season with salt and pepper. Transfer to the slow cooker, cover and cook on High for 3–4 hours until the peas are very soft.

3 Leave the soup to cool a little, then whiz half the soup in a blender or food processor until smooth. Pour the soup into a pan and reheat, then add the ham and check the seasoning. Ladle into warmed bowls and sprinkle with cracked black pepper to serve.

Cook's Tip
Dried peas form the base of this comforting soup. First, you need to soak them overnight in about 1 litre (1¾ pints) cold water. If you forget, put them straight into a pan with the water, bring to the boil and cook for 1–2 minutes, then leave to stand for 2 hours before using.

Without a Slow Cooker
At the end of step 2, leave the soup in the pan, reduce the heat and simmer, covered, for 45 minutes–1 hour or until the peas are very soft. Complete the recipe as directed from step 3.

Mexican Bean Soup

Serves 6
Preparation Time
15 minutes
Cooking Time
10 minutes in pan
then 2–3 hours
on High

Per Serving
(without lime butter)
184 calories
8g fat
(of which 1g saturates)
21g carbohydrate
1.3g salt

Vegetarian
Gluten Free

4 tbsp olive oil
1 onion, chopped
2 garlic cloves, chopped
pinch of crushed red chillies
1 tsp ground coriander
1 tsp ground cumin
½ tsp ground cinnamon
600ml (1 pint) hot vegetable stock
(see Cook's Tip, page 69)
300ml (½ pint) tomato juice
1–2 tsp chilli sauce
2 × 400g cans red kidney beans, drained and rinsed
2 tbsp freshly chopped coriander
salt and ground black pepper
fresh coriander leaves, roughly torn, to garnish
lime butter (optional, see Cook's Tip) and crusty
bread to serve

1 Heat the oil in a large pan. Add the onion, garlic, chillies and spices and fry gently for 5 minutes or until lightly golden.

2 Add the hot stock, the tomato juice, chilli sauce and beans and bring to the boil, then transfer to the slow cooker, cover and cook on High for 2–3 hours.

3 Leave the soup to cool a little, then whiz in batches in a blender or food processor until very smooth. Pour the soup into a pan, stir in the chopped coriander and heat through, then season to taste with salt and pepper.

4 Ladle the soup into warmed bowls. Top each portion with a few slices of lime butter, if you like, and scatter with torn coriander leaves. Serve with crusty bread.

Cook's Tip
Lime Butter Beat the grated zest and juice of ½ lime into 50g (2oz) softened butter and season to taste with salt and pepper. Shape into a log, wrap in clingfilm and chill until needed. To serve, unwrap and slice thinly.

Without a Slow Cooker
At the end of step 2, leave the mixture in the pan and bring to the boil. Reduce the heat, cover the pan and simmer gently for 20 minutes. Complete the recipe as directed from step 3.

Chocolate & Hazelnut Meringues

Serves 6
Preparation Time
25 minutes, plus
softening
Cooking Time
2 hours 10 minutes,
plus cooling

Per Serving
520 calories
42g fat
(of which 19g saturates)
32g carbohydrate
0.1g salt

Vegetarian
Gluten Free

125g (4oz) hazelnuts
125g (4oz) caster sugar
75g (3oz) plain chocolate
(at least 70% cocoa solids)
2 medium egg whites
300ml (½ pint) double cream
redcurrants, blackberries and
chocolate shavings to decorate
physalis (Cape gooseberries)
dipped in caramel (see Cook's Tip)
to serve (optional)

1 Preheat the oven to 110°C (90°C fan oven) mark ¼ and preheat the grill. Line two baking sheets with non-stick baking parchment. Spread the hazelnuts over a baking sheet. Toast under the hot grill until golden brown, turning them frequently. Put the hazelnuts into a clean teatowel and rub off the skins then put the nuts into a food processor with 3 tbsp of the sugar and process to a fine powder. Add the chocolate and pulse until roughly chopped.

2 Put the egg whites into a clean, grease-free bowl and whisk until stiff. Whisk in the remaining sugar, a spoonful at a time, until the mixture is stiff and shiny. Fold in the nut mixture.

3 Spoon the mixture on to the prepared baking sheets, making small rough mounds about 9cm (3½in) in diameter. Bake for about 45 minutes until the meringues will just peel off the paper. Gently push in the base of each meringue to form a deep hollow, then put back in the oven for 1¼ hours or until crisp and dry. Leave to cool.

4 Whip the cream until it just holds its shape; spoon three-quarters on to the meringues. Leave in the fridge to soften for up to 2 hours.

5 Decorate the meringues with the remaining cream, fruit and chocolate shavings. Serve immediately, with caramel-dipped physalis, if you like.

Cook's Tip
To make the caramel, dissolve 125g (4oz) caster sugar in a small heavy-based pan over a low heat. Bring to the boil and bubble until a golden caramel colour. Dip each physalis into the caramel, then place on an oiled baking sheet and cool.

Get Ahead
To prepare ahead Complete the recipe to the end of step 3, then store the meringues in an airtight container for up to one week.
To use Complete the recipe.

Orange & Chocolate Cheesecake

Serves 4	225g (8oz) chilled unsalted butter,
Preparation Time	plus extra to grease
45 minutes	250g (9oz) plain flour, sifted
Cooking Time	150g (5oz) light muscovado sugar
2–2¼ hours,	3 tbsp cocoa powder
plus cooling	chocolate curls to decorate (see Cook's Tip)

Per Serving	**For the topping**
767 calories	2 oranges
60g fat	800g (1lb 12oz) cream cheese
(of which 37g saturates)	250g (9oz) mascarpone cheese
53g carbohydrate	4 large eggs
1.2g salt	225g (8oz) golden caster sugar
	2 tbsp cornflour
Vegetarian	½ tsp vanilla extract
	1 vanilla pod

1 Preheat the oven to 180°C (160°C fan oven) mark 4. Grease a 23cm (9in) springform cake tin and base-line with baking parchment.

2 Cut 175g (6oz) butter into cubes. Melt the remaining butter and put to one side. Put the flour and cubed butter into a food processor with the sugar and cocoa powder. Whiz until the texture of fine breadcrumbs. (Alternatively, rub the butter into the flour in a large bowl by hand or using a pastry blender. Stir in the sugar and cocoa.) Pour in the melted butter and pulse, or stir with a fork, until the mixture comes together.

3 Spoon the crumb mixture into the prepared tin and press evenly on to the base, using the back of a metal spoon to level the surface. Bake for 35–40 minutes until lightly puffed; avoid over-browning or the biscuit base will have a bitter flavour. Remove from the oven and leave to cool. Reduce the oven temperature to 150°C (130°C fan oven) mark 2.

4 Meanwhile, make the topping. Grate the zest from the oranges, then squeeze the juice – you will need 150ml (¼ pint). Put the cream cheese, mascarpone, eggs, sugar, cornflour, grated orange zest and vanilla extract into a large bowl. Using a hand-held electric whisk, beat the ingredients together thoroughly until well combined.

5 Split the vanilla pod in half lengthways and, using the tip of a sharp knife, scrape out the seeds and add them to the cheese mixture. Beat in the orange juice and continue whisking until the mixture is smooth.

6 Pour the cheese mixture over the cooled biscuit base. Bake for about 1½ hours or until pale golden on top, slightly risen and just set around the edge. The cheesecake should still be slightly wobbly in the middle; it will set as it cools. Turn off the oven and leave the cheesecake inside, with the door ajar, to cool for 1 hour. Remove and leave to cool completely (about 3 hours), then chill.

7 Just before serving, unclip the tin and transfer the cheesecake to a plate. Scatter chocolate curls on top to decorate, if you like.

Cook's Tip
To make chocolate curls, melt the chocolate, then spread it out in a thin layer on a marble slab or clean worksurface. Leave to firm up. Using a sharp, flat-ended blade, scrape through the chocolate at a 45-degree angle.

Fruity Rice Pudding

Serves 6
Preparation Time
10 minutes
Cooking Time
2–3 hours on Low,
plus cooling and
chilling (optional)

Per Serving
323 calories
17g fat
(of which 10g saturates)
36g carbohydrate
0.2g salt

Vegetarian
Gluten Free

125g (4oz) short-grain pudding rice
1.1 litres (2 pints) full-fat milk
1 tsp vanilla extract
3–4 tbsp caster sugar
200ml (7fl oz) whipping cream
6 tbsp wild lingonberry sauce

1 Put the rice into the slow cooker with the milk, vanilla extract and sugar. Cover and cook on Low for 2–3 hours. You can enjoy the pudding hot now or leave to cool and continue the recipe.

2 Lightly whip the cream and fold through the pudding. Chill for 1 hour.

3 Divide the rice mixture among six glass dishes and top with 1 tbsp lingonberry sauce.

Try Something Different
For an alternative presentation, serve in tumblers, layering the rice pudding with the fruit sauce; you will need to use double the amount of fruit sauce.

Without a Slow Cooker
Put the rice into a pan with 600ml (1 pint) cold water. Bring to the boil, then reduce the heat and simmer until the liquid has evaporated. Add the milk, bring to the boil, then reduce the heat and simmer for 45 minutes until soft and creamy. Leave to cool, then complete the recipe from step 2.

Cranberry Christmas Pudding

Serves 12	200g (7oz) currants	1 tsp mixed spice
Preparation Time	200g (7oz) sultanas	175g (6oz) light
20 minutes,	200g (7oz) raisins	vegetarian suet
plus soaking	75g (3oz) dried	100g (3½oz) dark
Cooking Time	cranberries or cherries	muscovado sugar
8½ hours	grated zest and juice	50g (2oz) blanched
	of 1 orange	almonds, roughly
Per Serving	50ml (2fl oz) rum	chopped
448 calories	50ml (2fl oz) brandy	2 medium eggs
17g fat	1–2 tsp Angostura	butter to grease
(of which 7g saturates)	bitters	fresh or frozen
68g carbohydrate	1 small apple, peeled	cranberries (thawed
0.3g salt	and grated	if frozen), fresh bay
	1 carrot, grated	leaves and icing sugar
Vegetarian	175g (6oz) fresh	to decorate
	breadcrumbs	Brandy Butter (see
	100g (3½oz) plain	Cook's Tip) to serve
	flour, sifted	

1 Put the dried fruit, orange zest and juice into a large bowl. Pour the rum, brandy and Angostura bitters over. Cover and leave to soak in a cool place for at least 1 hour or overnight.

2 Add the apple, carrot, breadcrumbs, flour, mixed spice, suet, sugar, almonds and eggs to the bowl of soaked fruit. Use a wooden spoon to mix everything together well. Grease a 1.8 litre (3¼ pint) pudding basin and line with a 60cm (24in) square piece of muslin. Spoon the mixture into the basin and flatten the surface. Gather the muslin up and over the top, twist and secure with string. Put the basin on an upturned heatproof saucer or trivet in the base of a large pan, then pour in enough boiling water to come halfway up the side of the basin. Cover with a tight-fitting lid and simmer for 6 hours. Keep the water topped up with more boiling water.

3 Remove the basin from the pan and leave to cool. When the pudding is cold, remove from the basin, then wrap it in clingfilm and a double layer of foil. Store in a cool, dry place for up to six months.

4 To reheat, steam for 2½ hours; check the water level every 40 minutes and top up if necessary. Leave the pudding in the pan, covered, to keep warm until needed. Decorate with cranberries and bay leaves, dust with icing sugar and serve with Brandy Butter.

Cook's Tip
Brandy Butter Put 125g (4oz) unsalted butter in a bowl and beat until very soft. Gradually beat in 125g (4oz) sieved light muscovado sugar until very light and fluffy, then beat in 6 tbsp brandy, a spoonful at a time. Cover and chill for at least 3 hours.

Rich Fruit Cake

Cuts into 16 slices

Preparation Time
30 minutes

Cooking Time
2½ hours,
plus cooling

Per Slice
277 calories
11g fat
(of which 6g saturates)
38g carbohydrate
0.2g salt

Vegetarian

175g (6oz) unsalted butter, cubed, plus extra
to grease
1kg (2¼lb) mixed dried fruit
100g (3½oz) ready-to-eat dried prunes,
roughly chopped
50g (2oz) ready-to-eat dried figs, roughly chopped
100g (3½oz) dried cranberries
2 balls preserved stem ginger in syrup, grated and
syrup reserved
grated zest and juice of 1 orange
175ml (6fl oz) brandy
2 splashes Angostura bitters
175g (6oz) dark muscovado sugar
200g (7oz) self-raising flour
½ tsp ground cinnamon
½ tsp freshly grated nutmeg
½ tsp ground cloves
4 medium eggs, beaten

1 Preheat the oven to 150°C (130°C fan oven) mark 2.
Grease a 20.5cm (8in) round, deep cake tin and line
the base and sides with greaseproof paper.

2 Put all the dried fruit into a very large pan and add
the ginger, 1 tbsp reserved ginger syrup, the orange
zest and juice, brandy and Angostura bitters. Bring to the
boil, then reduce the heat and simmer for 5 minutes. Add
the butter and sugar and heat gently to melt. Stir
occasionally until the sugar dissolves. Take the pan off
the heat and leave to cool for a couple of minutes.

3 Add the flour, spices and beaten eggs and mix well.
Pour the mixture into the prepared tin and level the
surface. Wrap the outside of the tin in brown paper and
secure with string to protect the cake during cooking.
Bake for 2–2½ hours – cover with greaseproof paper after
about 1½ hours – until the cake is firm to the touch and a
skewer inserted into the centre comes out clean.

4 Cool in the tin for 2-3 hours, then remove from the
tin, leaving the greaseproof paper on, transfer to a
wire rack and leave to cool completely. Wrap the cake in
a layer of clingfilm, then in foil.

Cook's Tip

Store in an airtight container. It will keep for up to three
months. If you like, after the cake has matured for two
weeks, prick it all over with a metal skewer and sprinkle
with 1 tbsp brandy. Leave to soak in, then rewrap and
store as before.

Winter Fruit Compote

Serves 6
Preparation Time
10 minutes
Cooking Time
5 minutes in pan
then 3–4 hours
on Low

Per Serving
139 calories
trace fat
26g carbohydrate
0.1g salt

Vegetarian
Gluten Free

75g (3oz) ready-to-eat dried pears
75g (3oz) ready-to-eat dried figs
75g (3oz) ready-to-eat dried apricots
75g (3oz) ready-to-eat prunes
1 star anise
½ cinnamon stick
300ml (½ pint) apple juice
300ml (½ pint) dry white wine
light muscovado sugar to taste
crème fraîche or thick Greek-style yogurt to serve

1 Put the dried fruits into the slow cooker with the star anise and cinnamon stick.

2 Put the apple juice and wine into a pan and bring to the boil. Pour over the fruit, cover and cook on Low for 3–4 hours until plump and tender.

3 Sprinkle the sugar over the fruit if you like, and serve the compote with crème fraîche or thick Greek-style yogurt.

Try Something Different
Replace the figs with dried apple rings and the pears with raisins.

Without a Slow Cooker
Put the dried fruits, spices, apple juice and wine in a pan and bring to the boil slowly. Reduce the heat, cover and simmer for 45 minutes until the fruits are plump and tender. Top up the liquid if necessary. Complete the recipe from step 3.

Index

KITCHEN NOTES

Both metric and imperial measures are given for the recipes. Follow either set of measures, not a mixture of both, as they are not interchangeable.

All spoon measures are level.
1 tsp = 5ml spoon; 1 tbsp = 15ml spoon.

Ovens and grills must be preheated to the specified temperature.

Medium eggs should be used except where otherwise specified. Free-range eggs are recommended.

Note that some recipes contain raw or lightly cooked eggs. The young, elderly, pregnant women and anyone with an immune-deficiency disease should avoid these because of the slight risk of salmonella.

Photographers: Neil Barclay (pages 19 and 62); Martin Brigdale (pages 86 and 87); Nicki Dowey (pages 6, 7, 8, 9, 10, 11, 12, 13, 14, 15, 17, 18, 20, 21, 22, 23, 27, 28, 29, 30, 31, 36, 37, 38, 39, 40, 41, 44, 45, 48, 49, 50, 51, 52, 53, 55, 56 ,57, 60, 61, 67, 68, 69, 70, 71, 72, 73, 78, 79, 80, 81, 82, 83, 88, 89, 90, 91, 92, 93 and 94); Fiona Kennedy (pages 26, 64 and 65); Craig Robertson (pages 5, 16, 24, 25, 32, 33, 42, 43, 54, 66, 74, 75, 76, 77, 84 and 85); Lucinda Symons (pages 34, 35, 46, 47, 58, 59 and 63)

Home Economists: Joanna Farrow, Emma Jane Frost, Teresa Goldfinch, Alice Hart, Lucy McKelvie, Kim Morphew, Aya Nishimura, Bridget Sargeson, Kate Trend and Mari Mererid Williams
Stylists: Tamzin Ferdinando, Wei Tang, Helen Trent and Fanny Ward

First published in Great Britain in 2012
by Collins & Brown
10 Southcombe Street
London W14 0RA

An imprint of Anova Books Company Ltd

The Good Housekeeping website is
www.allaboutyou.com/goodhousekeeping

ISBN 978-1-908449-27-6

A catalogue record for this book is available from the British Library.

Reproduction by Dot Gradations Ltd, UK
Printed and bound by 1010 Printing International Ltd, China

This book can be ordered direct from the publisher. Contact the marketing department, but try your bookshop first.

www.anovabooks.com